T0358345

Cambridge Elements

Elements in the Philosophy of Friedrich Nietzsche
edited by
Kaitlyn Creasy
California State University, San Bernardino
Matthew Meyer
The University of Scranton

NIETZSCHE ON THE ETERNAL RECURRENCE

Neil Sinhababu
National University of Singapore

CAMBRIDGE
UNIVERSITY PRESS

Shaftesbury Road, Cambridge CB2 8EA, United Kingdom

One Liberty Plaza, 20th Floor, New York, NY 10006, USA

477 Williamstown Road, Port Melbourne, VIC 3207, Australia

314–321, 3rd Floor, Plot 3, Splendor Forum, Jasola District Centre,
New Delhi – 110025, India

103 Penang Road, #05–06/07, Visioncrest Commercial, Singapore 238467

Cambridge University Press is part of Cambridge University Press & Assessment,
a department of the University of Cambridge.

We share the University's mission to contribute to society through the pursuit of
education, learning and research at the highest international levels of excellence.

www.cambridge.org
Information on this title: www.cambridge.org/9781009517478

DOI: 10.1017/9781009443180

First published 2024

A catalogue record for this publication is available from the British Library

ISBN 978-1-009-51747-8 Hardback
ISBN 978-1-009-44321-0 Paperback
ISSN 2976-5722 (online)
ISSN 2976-5714 (print)

Nietzsche on the Eternal Recurrence

Elements in the Philosophy of Friedrich Nietzsche

DOI: 10.1017/9781009443180
First published online: December 2024

Neil Sinhababu
National University of Singapore

Author for correspondence: Neil Sinhababu, neiladri@gmail.com

Abstract: The idea of the eternal recurrence is that everyone will live the exact same lives again an infinite number of times. Nietzsche appreciates that this would multiply the value of a single life by infinity, justifying intense emotional responses. His unpublished notes provide a cosmological argument for the eternal recurrence that anticipates Poincaré's recurrence theorem. Nietzsche's *Thus Spoke Zarathustra* describes its hero discovering this idea and struggling to accept the recurrence of all bad things. He eventually comes to love the eternal recurrence because it will bring back all the joys of his life, and teaches this idea to others.

Keywords: Nietzsche, eternal recurrence, *Thus Spoke Zarathustra*, cosmology, value

ISBNs: 9781009517478 (HB), 9781009443210 (PB), 9781009443180 (OC)
ISSNs: 2976-5722 (online), 2976-5714 (print)

Contents

1 The Introduction of Infinities

Looking back on his life's work in *Ecce Homo*, Friedrich Nietzsche lavishes extraordinary praise on *Thus Spoke Zarathustra*. He says, "Among my writings my *Zarathustra* stands to my mind by itself. With that I have given mankind the greatest present that has ever been made to it so far" (EH "Pref" 4). He later describes the "fundamental conception of this work, the idea of the eternal recurrence, this highest formula of affirmation that is at all attainable" (EH "Books" Z:1). The eternal recurrence is so significant because it could give our worldly existence infinite value.

Suppose our lives eternally recur, meaning that we have lived an infinity of identical lives in the past, and will live an infinity more in the future. This can easily give infinite positive or negative value to anyone's total existence over eternity. If your life is good overall, living it infinite times is infinitely good. If your life is bad overall, living it infinite times is infinitely bad. In Nietzsche's search for value in the world after the death of God, these infinities of value – both positive and negative – are a tremendous discovery.

There is considerable scholarly debate about whether Nietzsche is really telling us that the universe is structured so that our lives will eternally recur. Alexander Nehamas (1985) argues that the eternal recurrence "has little if anything to do with the nature of the universe" (6).[1] Recent scholarship largely joins Nehamas in taking the eternal recurrence not to be a cosmological hypothesis, but a way to investigate evaluative questions.

Nehamas offers two widely shared reasons to deny that Nietzsche offers a cosmological hypothesis. First, Nietzsche doesn't directly assert that everything will eternally recur anywhere in the published works. In *Zarathustra* such assertions occur only in dreams, visions, and speeches by talking animals. Its protagonist Zarathustra never confidently asserts that the eternal recurrence will happen, except perhaps in a whisper unheard by readers. Outside *Zarathustra*, the most explicit published discussion of the eternal recurrence is in *Gay Science* 341, where a demon proclaims it in a thought-experiment. There and elsewhere, Nietzsche focuses on the psychological health of those who can happily accept the eternal recurrence, rather than the arguments for it. His clearest cosmological arguments for the eternal recurrence are in *Will to Power* 1066 / KSA 11:38[12], which as an unpublished note may not represent his settled views.

---

[1] Sharing Nehamas' doubts are Soll (1973), Strong (1975), Higgins (1987), Magnus (1978), Clark (1990), Solomon (2003), Welshon (2004), Anderson (2005), Reginster (2006), Leiter (2019), and Huddleston (2022).

Second, Nietzsche's cosmological arguments for eternal recurrence are unsound. While many empirical objections are available, perhaps the most straightforward arises from astronomical evidence suggesting a perpetually expanding universe.[2] An irreversible and eternal expansion prevents any return to previous states. Many interpreters therefore join Nehamas in not committing Nietzsche to the idea that the universe will recur eternally, perhaps regarding this interpretation as charitable.

Scholars downplaying the cosmology might be surprised to discover historians of statistical mechanics describing the eternal recurrence as a predecessor to Henri Poincaré's (1890) recurrence theorem. Juliano Neves (2019) notes that two assumptions Nietzsche suggests in KSA 11:38[12] – finite and conserved forces, and infinite time – enable Poincaré to show that nearly all states of the universe will recur. He writes that "Nietzsche works in the same direction as Poincaré" (191), and notes that Nietzsche's insight preceded Poincaré's theorem. In his scientific biography of Poincaré, Ferdinand Verhulst (2012) treats Nietzsche as a predecessor and quotes the demon of *GS* 341. Stephen Brush (1976) spends three pages discussing Nietzsche in his two-volume history of the kinetic theory of gases. He writes, "The suggestion that eternal recurrence might be proved as a theorem of physics, rather than as a religious or philosophical doctrine, seems to have occurred at about the same time to the German philosopher Friedrich Nietzsche and the French physicist Henri Poincaré" (628).[3]

Brush treats "Nietzsche's effort as a qualitative anticipation of Poincaré's theorem" (629). Both proceed from the same two premises and conclude that present arrangements must eternally recur. While they make different assumptions about determinism and other issues, these assumptions aren't necessary for our lives to recur an infinite number of times. Brush therefore distinguishes Nietzsche and Poincaré from predecessors who suggested recurrence without a similar argument.[4]

Even if more recent evidence makes the eternal recurrence extremely unlikely, Poincaré's theorem shows that the evidence of the late 1800s left it plausible enough for genuine scientific consideration. As Nietzsche's idea of the eternal recurrence anticipates an important scientific discovery, interpretive charity can't oppose treating it as a scientific hypothesis and may favor doing so. This suggests regarding Nietzsche's cosmological discussions as essential to the idea, as Lawrence Hatab (2005), Paul Loeb (2010), and Robin Small (2010) have rightly done.[5]

---

[2] Frieman, Turner, and Huterer (2008).
[3] Brush refers to Pfeffer (1965). D'Iorio (2014) recognizes the connection to Poincaré.
[4] Jenkins (2012) discusses Nietzsche's relation to Heraclitus and the Stoics. Mollison (2021) emphasizes differences between them.
[5] Also Danto (1965), Kaufmann (1968), Zuboff (1973), Krueger (1978), and Meyer (2022).

Nietzsche's early published presentations of the eternal recurrence in *The Gay Science* and *Zarathustra*, written in the first half of the 1880s, occur in hypothetical scenarios or fiction. This makes sense if Nietzsche wrote them with genuine uncertainty about whether the eternal recurrence would happen in our world. A credence intermediate between belief and disbelief is natural toward scientific hypotheses strongly suggested by some considerations, and requiring further plausible but hard-to-verify assumptions. Uncertainty likely prevented Nietzsche from discussing the eternal recurrence more fully in print. He didn't want to present it explicitly and publicly as a factual thesis without a stronger argument, and he realized that he couldn't make the argument himself. That would require Poincaré's scientific talents, and eventually the mathematical talents of Constantin Carathéodory (1919), who finalized a proof of the recurrence theorem using measure theory.

Nietzsche knew that proving a recurrence theorem as Poincaré and Carathéodory did was beyond his abilities. He instead chose a reasonable alternative for an extraordinarily creative person. He wrote science fiction in which talking animals proclaim the eternal recurrence.[6]

Science fiction often envisions scientific possibilities to consider their consequences for life. *Star Trek* envisions how space travel might let us encounter alien societies. William Gibson's *Neuromancer* envisions how the internet might transform our society. *Bill and Ted's Excellent Adventure* envisions how time travel might permit comical interactions with historical figures. GS 341 and *Zarathustra* envision how the eternal recurrence might affect the value of our existence, and how we might feel about it. GS 341 describes intense emotions toward the eternal recurrence, which *Zarathustra* dramatizes.

Nietzsche's uncertainty about the eternal recurrence makes *Zarathustra* especially good for discussing it. The physical laws in *Zarathustra* resemble ours but may differ slightly. Its world has flying men, fire hounds living in volcanoes, and animals that talk. If eternal recurrence doesn't happen in our universe due to endless cosmic expansion or some other empirical contingency, it might still happen in the fictional universe of *Zarathustra*.

Nietzsche's confidence in the eternal recurrence might have increased by the end of his career. The unpublished note KSA 11:38[12], published in 1888, uses the same two premises as Poincaré in a clear and nonfictional argument for recurrence. Nietzsche occasionally remarks positively on eternal recurrence in his works of 1888. Thomas Brobjer (2023) finds evidence from Nietzsche's notes that he planned to defend this cosmology explicitly in a future masterwork.

---

[6] Nietzsche likely regarded acceptance of the eternal recurrence as pragmatically beneficial overall, even if it turned out to be false. See Soll (1973), Magnus (1978), and Clark (1990).

While Nietzsche clearly retained interest in the eternal recurrence and sharpened his thoughts about a cosmological argument for it, it's less clear how he thought about it in the late 1880s than in the early 1880s. Unpublished notes, unrealized plans, and passing mentions are weaker evidence about Nietzsche's confident and considered views than extended published discussions. This Element therefore focuses mainly on discussions in the early published works – *Gay Science* and especially *Zarathustra*. KSA 11:38[12] however deserves close consideration, as his most straightforward argument for the eternal recurrence. Also deserving attention is KSA 11:11[141], his first unpublished note about it. Written on the first day the eternal recurrence occurred to him, this note shows that he immediately recognized the infinities of value it would generate.

Scholarly discussion of the eternal recurrence often categorizes some interpretations as cosmological, and others as broadly evaluative including attitudinal or normative interpretations suggesting evaluations of attitudes and actions. As Bevis McNeil (2020) notes, these categories are not exclusive. They offer right answers to different questions. Cosmological interpretations are right about what the eternal recurrence is. Evaluative interpretations are right about why Nietzsche is interested in it. Nietzsche defines the eternal recurrence as a cosmological doctrine, writing "The doctrine of the 'eternal recurrence' – that is, of the unconditional and infinitely repeated circular course of all things" (EH "Books" BT:3). This doctrine interests Nietzsche because of its evaluative significance for our attitudes, our actions, and our existence. The climax of *Zarathustra* doesn't involve a proof that the universe will eternally recur, but rather a song expressing love of life, with each of seven verses ending "*For I love you, O eternity!*" (Z IV: "Seven Seals").

The next two sections respectively address the evaluative significance of the eternal recurrence and the cosmological arguments for it. Section 2 discusses early statements of the eternal recurrence, especially from the demon of GS 341. Nietzsche describes the intense emotions we might feel upon seeing the infinities of value it introduces. Section 3 compares the argument for recurrence in KSA 11:38[12] with Poincaré's theorem. Both proceed from similar assumptions and raise issues related to the second law of thermodynamics, though Nietzsche's well-ordered cycles of recurrence require an additional deterministic assumption. These two sections respectively discuss Nietzsche's earliest (1881–1882) and latest (1888) writings about the eternal recurrence.

The last ten sections tell the story of the eternal recurrence in *Zarathustra*. Its hero is initially overwhelmed by the infinite negative value introduced by the eternal recurrence. But after going into solitude and reflecting on life,

Zarathustra joyously accepts the eternal recurrence for its infinity of positive value.

Zarathustra only comes to grasp the idea of the eternal recurrence slowly, and initially reacts to it with very negative emotions. Section 4 begins by discussing "The Soothsayer," where a soothsayer's dark prophecy of eternally meaningless life gives Zarathustra a symbolic dream about the eternal recurrence that he doesn't understand. He dreams of observing the vast lifeless periods in the cycle of recurrence as a night watchman in death's castle, until a coffin bursts open and life emerges again. Section 5 describes how the idea first emerges into Zarathustra's conscious thought in "On Redemption," as he concludes a speech about how bad events in the past frustrate the will. He is shocked into speechlessness as he realizes that all bad events will recur eternally. Section 6 describes Zarathustra's struggle to even speak of the resulting infinite negative value in "The Stillest Hour" and the sections surrounding it. Commanded by a mysterious voice, he journeys home toward the solitude of his mountain cave to gather the emotional strength to confront the idea.

Eventually, Zarathustra finds the courage to face the abysmal thought of infinite negative value. Section 7 considers his first public statement about the eternal recurrence in "The Vision and the Riddle," which describes a vision in which he and a malicious dwarf consider how the infinite line of time will continue after passing through the gateway of the moment. He then has a vision of how he will overcome his horror at infinite negative value, symbolized by a shepherd biting the head off a snake that has crawled into his mouth. Section 8 describes Zarathustra's emotional struggle with this abysmal thought in "The Convalescent," which leaves him bedridden for a week. His animals proclaim the eternal recurrence as he recovers.

As Zarathustra recognizes infinite positive value introduced by the eternal recurrence, *Zarathustra* becomes a love story between its protagonist and Life. Section 9 discusses "The Other Dancing Song," where Zarathustra dances with Life. At the end Life is sad that he will soon leave her, and he whispers into her ear that he will return. Section 10 discusses the song concluding this section, "Once More," which describes the vast magnitudes of time, woe, and joy in the cosmology of recurrence. Section 11 discusses "The Seven Seals," where Zarathustra sings seven verses about why he loves his life so much and wants it to eternally recur. Each verse concludes by expressing his wish to marry Eternity, whose maiden name is Life.

The rest of the Element describes how Zarathustra invites nine "higher men" to his cave, and teaches them to wish for recurrence. Section 12 discusses the first of these higher men, the soothsayer with the dark prophecy of eternally meaningless life. Many others arrive, wishing to live with Zarathustra, though he offers them only dinner and a night's stay. Section 13 discusses "The Ass Festival," where the higher men worship a donkey, and offer a convincing naturalistic defense of doing so. As the night ends, the soothsayer and perhaps the donkey dance with drunken joy, and the higher men express a wish for recurrence by singing "Once More."

Zarathustra tells the story of how a philosopher fell in love with Eternity. Poincaré, Carathéodory, and modern physics tell Eternity's side of the story. In explaining the science, and explicating the narrative and poetry of *Zarathustra*, this Element aims to tell as much of the whole story as it can.

2 *Gay Science* 341, "The Greatest Weight," Considers Infinite Value

The Gay Science, published in 1882, is Nietzsche's first book discussing eternal recurrence. He first alludes to it in a section titled "Let us beware" which warns against anthropomorphizing the universe: "The whole musical box repeats eternally its tune which may never be called a melody" (GS 109). His early unpublished notes on the eternal recurrence similarly emphasize that it doesn't aim at any value or result from any intention, sometimes using the same words: "Let us beware of attributing any kind of striving to this circuit" and that "rationality or irrationality are not predicates for the universe" (CWFN 6 (357), KSA 9:11[157]). Nietzsche rejects these anthropomorphisms for the same naturalistic reasons he rejects religion, writing that "The modern-scientific counterpart to faith in God is faith in the *universe as organism*: this disgusts me" (CWFN 6 (374), KSA 9:11[201]).

As Matthew Meyer (2022) describes, GS 109 confirms that Nietzsche thought of the eternal recurrence cosmologically from the beginning:

> First, we can connect the title of GS 109 to at least three notes from this time in which this phrase is used, and, in these notes, Nietzsche formulates the eternal recurrence in cosmological terms (KSA 9:11[157], [201], [202]). Second, Paulo D'Iorio has shown that Nietzsche first encountered this phrase, "let us beware," in Eugen Dühring's *Course of Philosophy*, and Dühring uses the phrase in the context of discussing questions about the beginning of the cosmos (2014: 74). Taken together, it becomes clear that the first mention of the eternal recurrence in Nietzsche's work should be understood cosmologically. (113)

As we'll see, regarding the eternal recurrence as a cosmological doctrine allows us to better understand its evaluative significance.

Nietzsche's classic statement of the eternal recurrence, later in the same book, connects the cosmology to its evaluative significance:

What if some day or night a demon were to steal after you into your loneliest loneliness and say to you: "This life as you now live it and have lived it, you will have to live once more and innumerable times more; and there will be nothing new in it, but every pain and every joy and every thought and sigh and everything unutterably small or great in your life will have to return to you, in the same succession and sequence – even this spider and this moonlight between the trees, and even this moment and I myself. The eternal hourglass of existence is turned upside down again and again, and you with it, speck of dust!" (GS 341)

Nietzsche then asks how you would emotionally respond if you knew your life would recur eternally: "Would you not throw yourself down and gnash your teeth and curse the demon who spoke thus? Or have you once experienced a tremendous moment when you would have answered him: 'You are a god and never have I heard anything more divine'" (GS 341).

Ivan Soll (1973) argues that "the prospect of the infinite repetition of the pleasure or pain of one's present life entailed by the doctrine of eternal recurrence should actually be a matter of complete indifference" (339). Kathleen Higgins (1987) similarly asks why the eternal recurrence would justify such intense emotional responses: "What difference does the doctrine of eternal recurrence make? Even if the theory of time it proposes were true, nothing in our lives would be any different" (163). Aaron Ridley (1997) also writes, "The thought of Eternal recurrence, then, should be a matter of the deepest indifference. Why *care*?" (20). Indeed, the eternal recurrence is largely inconsequential for one's current life. Perhaps it favors living a short but wonderful life rather than a longer life with less concentrated satisfactions. If you're guaranteed an infinite amount of life, making it all wonderful rather than merely okay overall might be best. But Nietzsche doesn't suggest living for a good time rather than a long time. He instead suggests that we might have intense positive or negative emotions.

Intense emotional responses make sense because the eternal recurrence infinitely multiplies the value of existence, adding infinite lives as good as the present one. If your life is good overall, that goodness is yours not just once, but infinite times over the course of eternity. If your life is bad overall, that badness too is infinitely repeated. Unless your life is exactly neutral in value, the eternal recurrence makes your total existence infinitely good or bad. Any value in life that can be summed over time becomes infinite – objective or subjective, moral or prudential, great or small. Many evaluative theories deliver this consequence. Utilitarians face an eternity with infinite net pleasure or infinite net displeasure, which they regard as infinitely good or bad.

The eternal recurrence matters like an eternal religious afterlife. Anyone whose life is good overall receives the infinite positive net value of heaven from the eternal recurrence. Anyone whose life is bad overall receives the infinite negative net value of hell. The eternal recurrence differs from these theological afterlives in offering a total existence that mixes happiness and suffering and dilutes them across time. But the net happiness or unhappiness it offers is nevertheless infinite like heaven or hell. These heavenly or hellish consequences answer Soll, Higgins, and Ridley's questions. Whether one has an afterlife of infinite happiness or suffering matters a great deal, even if one learns nothing new about how one's earthly life will go.

The value of things determines how intense our emotional responses to them should be.[7] We should be delighted by very good things, which are often called delightful. We should be horrified by very bad things, which are often called horrible. Things of lesser goodness and badness should arouse weaker feelings. The close connection between evaluative and emotional terms testifies to how feelings represent value, and how value justifies feelings. If the intensity that feelings should have is proportional to the value of their objects, infinite value demands infinitely intense feelings.

As finite beings, humans can't have infinitely intense feelings or distinct thoughts about each of an infinite number of things. While mathematicians like Georg Cantor can mentally represent many concepts of infinity, they do so only in terms of relations between these infinities and other numbers, rather than by having distinct thoughts about each of an infinite series of elements. Furthermore, the phenomenological, motivational, and physiological dimensions of human emotion are finite. Good news can't make us feel infinite joy, infuriating news can't motivate us with infinite wrathful fury, and sad news can't make us cry infinite tears.

Our feelings can however shift toward infinite intensity simply by getting stronger. Our strongest feelings toward the eternal recurrence will be most apt, as they come closest to infinite intensity. Those whose lives are bad overall might curse the demon upon learning that their total existence will be infinitely bad. Those whose lives are good overall might call the demon a god, being blessed with infinite value like that of heaven.

Paul Loeb (2018) interprets Nietzsche as claiming that we can have infinitely intense experiences within a single moment. He writes that "GS 341 is concerned to describe my experience of the infinitely repeated moment as happening only during this very moment itself in the midst of my present embodied life in this current cycle" (434). This might involve one's consciousness dividing

---

[7] Tappolet (2016) and Mitchell (2021).

into infinite identical consciousnesses, each with identical qualia corresponding to the infinity of moments identical to this one. Loeb sees this as how "I am actually reliving this revelatory moment countless times during this moment itself" (434) and having an "immanent experience of eternal recurrence" (435). Unfortunately, humans are psychologically incapable of experiencing a whole infinity of identical moments at once, and Nietzschean psychology excludes such supernatural powers. Moreover, it's unclear why the demon's remarks about the entire sequence and series of moments returning would trigger infinite experiences of that one moment. The demon describes eternal recurrence, and Loeb suggests instantaneous infinite co-occurrence.

Paul Katsafanas (2022) notes that the eternal recurrence shouldn't change whether we say "yes" or "no" to existence. As he writes, "If suffering is not an objection to living once, it should not be an objection to living twice, five times, or an infinite number of times." Moreover, "while the total amount of suffering would be increased as lives are multiplied, the ratio of suffering to whatever one sees as redeeming suffering would remain constant" (67). But if ratios determine whether to prefer existence, total amounts determine how intensely to prefer it. While the eternal recurrence doesn't change whether to prefer existence, it adds that this preference should be infinitely strong. Whether to say "yes" or "no" to existence may be less important than whether to add infinite exclamation marks. Finite values change more when multiplied by infinity than when multiplied by -1.

The eternal recurrence gives our actions infinite weight, as any value associated with them and their consequences becomes infinite with eternal repetition. Making the titular reference of the section, Nietzsche writes, "The question in each and every thing, 'Do you desire this once more and innumerable times more?' would lie upon your actions as the greatest weight" (GS 341). The consequences of every action for one's life are experienced not only once, but infinitely many times, making decisions of what to do infinitely important.

Nietzsche recognized that the eternal recurrence would generate infinities of value from the day he first thought of it. He recalls writing a first note about it "in August 1881: it was penned on a sheet with the notation underneath: '6000 feet beyond man and time.' That day I was walking through the woods along the lake of Silvaplana; at a powerful pyramidal rock not far from Surlei I stopped. It was then that this idea came to me" (EH "Books" Z:1.) This note states its date and location as "Beginning of August 1881 in Sils-Maria, 6000 feet above sea level and much higher above all human affairs" (CWFN 6 351, KSA 9:11[141]). Sils Maria is within an hour's walk of the pyramidal rock, so Nietzsche likely went home and wrote this note just hours after first thinking of the idea. It introduces the idea with a similar metaphor as the title of GS 341: "The new *weight: the eternal recurrence of the same*" (CWFN 6 350, KSA 9:11[141]).

Nietzsche's next remark expresses his immediate recognition that the eternal recurrence generates infinities of value: "Infinite importance of our knowing, erring, our habits, lifestyles for everything coming." Seeing the mathematical consequences as utilitarians might, he writes, "an absolute excess of joy must be demonstrated, otherwise the choice is the annihilation of our self with respect to humankind as a means of annihilating humankind. Even this; we have to place the past, ours and that of all humankind, on the scale and also outweigh it" (CWFN 6 351, KSA 9:11[141]). If the total joy in one cycle of recurrence exceeds the total woe, the net joy in all of reality will be infinite. But if the total suffering exceeds the total joy, the net suffering will be infinite. Annihilating everything would then be preferable as it would raise the value of everything from negative infinity to zero. As noted when the idea first surfaces in *Zarathustra*, it is also impossible as whatever has already happened of our lives would still recur eternally.

Historical suffering may exceed historical happiness, leading to Nietzsche reject this utilitarian approach: " – no! this piece of humankind's history *will* and must eternally repeat – *this* we may exclude from the bottom line, on this we have no influence: though it immediately burdens our empathy and prejudices us against life generally" (CWFN 6 351, KSA 9:11[141]). Life becomes impossible to affirm not only for those with more suffering than joy, but for compassionate people who pity them – "In order not to be toppled by this, our compassion must not be great." To Nietzsche, "whether *we* still *want to live* is the question: and how!" (CWFN 6 352, KSA 9:11[141]).

Another unpublished note from 1881 describes the significance of regarding ourselves as having "eternal souls and eternal becoming and future self betterment":

> My teaching says: the task is to live your life in such a way that you have to wish to live again – you will in any case. To he whom striving gives the highest feeling, let him strive; to he whom repose gives the highest feeling, let him rest; to he whom ordering, following, obedience give the highest feeling, let him obey. Only may he become aware of what gives him the highest feeling and he recoils back before nothing! Eternity is at stake! (KSA 9:11[163]).[8]

Here Nietzsche emphasizes the practical significance of the eternal recurrence – we should live so that we wish to live again. Since the cosmology of recurrence guarantees that we will live the same lives for eternity, the stakes are infinitely high. This is the "weight" that GS 341 and KSA 9:11[141] describe.

---

[8] Ansell-Pearson (1991).

The arrangement of good and bad events in time helps to address puzzles arising when positive and negative infinities combine. All joys over eternity have infinite positive value and all woes over eternity have infinite negative value, suggesting an overall value of infinity minus infinity, which is mathematically undefined.[9] Rather than suggesting that you would curse the demon or proclaim him a god, this suggests being very confused about the undefined value of your eternal existence. But the temporal ordering of these joys and woes ensures better-defined total amounts. If one's life is good, the total value of one's existence starting at any time and continuing forever into the past or future will be a well-defined positive infinity. Any continuous period of time that consists entirely of whole lives, which are natural units of existence for ethical evaluation, will have positive value.

Infinities of value can be avoided by restricting additivity, perhaps with a limit on the total value that any specific type of good thing can add to one's total existence. But if a happy day improves one's life, why wouldn't a second identical happy day similarly improve one's life? While preferring novelty might make us value the second identical happy day less, this preference makes less sense if we can't remember the first happy day. Since we won't remember good things from a previous life, they will seem just as new to us when they recur in our present lives.

Pascal's Wager illustrates the significance of infinite value even under uncertainty. Pascal argues that the infinite heavenly reward awaiting believers pragmatically justifies belief in God, even if the probability of God and heaven existing seems low. Even a low probability of truth multiplied by the infinite value of eternal happiness gives religious belief infinite expected value. A small probability of infinite gain means a great deal to decision-theoretically rational agents. Nietzsche doesn't use this in a pragmatic argument for believing in the eternal recurrence, as it occurs independently of whether one believes. But as Pascal's Wager indicates, even a low probability of the eternal recurrence would matter a great deal to him.

Religious believers may have additional reasons to feel strongly about the eternal recurrence. If this life is eternal, eternal reward and punishment in the afterlife can never begin. Those who hoped for heaven might curse the demon as they learn that they won't get it, and those whose lives are bad overall might curse the loudest.[10] Those who feared hell might be more sanguine, especially if they see their earthly lives as good overall. The eternal recurrence similarly displaces divine creation by leaving no beginning for God to create the universe. It displaces a divine heaven, hell, and creator all at once.

---

[9] For discussions of how decision theory might deal with such infinities, see Askell (2018), Wilkinson (2023), and Goodsell (forthcoming).

[10] Reginster (2006).

Nietzsche's discussions of the eternal recurrence often end on a positive note, as GS 341 does. He asks, "how well disposed would you have to become to yourself and to life *to crave nothing more fervently* than this ultimate eternal confirmation and seal?" Someone who loves life might indeed crave infinite life more than anything else. As we'll see, this is how Zarathustra's love of life becomes love of eternity.

3 The Argument of KSA 11:38[12] Anticipates Poincaré's Theorem

A paragraph in Nietzsche's unpublished notebook entry KSA 11:38[12] / *Will to Power* 1066 makes an empirical argument for the eternal recurrence, suggesting the same two premises as Poincaré's recurrence theorem. The first premise is that matter can occupy only a finite range of physical states, which Nietzsche defends by appealing to the conservation of matter and energy. The second premise is that time is infinite. Nietzsche and Poincaré both conclude from versions of these assumptions that physical systems will return to each of their earlier states an infinite number of times.

Written in the spring of 1888, this note is one of Nietzsche's last and most substantial discussions of the eternal recurrence. He and his mental health collapsed in the streets of Turin on January 3, 1889. Severe dementia prevented him from doing philosophy until his death in 1900.

The timing is tragic. Poincaré's theorem was revealed to the world on January 21, 1889 with considerable media fanfare, after winning King Oscar of Sweden's prize competition. With another month of sanity, Nietzsche might have learned of Poincaré's theorem. For his part, Poincaré doesn't seem to have ever encountered Nietzsche's writings on the issue.

In historical work focused on Poincaré and his scientific contemporaries, Stephen Brush (1976) and Ferdinand Verhulst (2012) note that Nietzsche's derivation of recurrence anticipates Poincaré's theorem.[11] While current science makes the eternal recurrence extremely unlikely as Nietzsche envisioned it, the resemblance to Poincaré's theorem reveals it to be a plausible hypothesis given the evidence of their time. Poincaré and his contemporaries applied the theorem to heat transfer, the motions of fluids and gases, and the solar system, and didn't focus on the recurrence of the whole universe. But the theorem applies to the whole universe too, if it has only finite possible states and exists for infinite time.

Brush states Poincaré's theorem as follows: "the group of measure-preserving transformations of the phase space resulting from the dynamical equations of

---

[11] Others noting this connection include Capek (1960), Small (1991), D'Iorio (2014), Small (2017), and in physics Carroll (2019).

motion has the property that almost all points in a set of positive measure are carried back into that set infinitely many times" (630–631). The phase space of a system represents its possible states. Measure-preserving dynamical systems are conservative systems, so called because all of phase space is conserved over time, meaning that states possible in the past can't become impossible in the future. All changes in conservative systems are reversible, with every past possibility forever remaining a future possibility. Poincaré's theorem holds in all conservative systems. It shows that in these systems, almost all possible states will recur infinitely many times over eternity.[12] Nonrecurring states are very rare, making up only an infinitesimal portion of phase space. So it is nearly certain that any past, present, or future state will recur.

Nietzsche begins by suggesting a finite set of possible states, by appealing to conservation laws concerning matter and energy: "If the world may be thought of as a certain definite quantity of force and as a certain definite number of centers of force – and every other representation remains indefinite and there-fore useless – it follows that, in the great dice game of existence, it must pass through a calculable number of combinations." (WP 1066 / KSA 11:38[12])

The reference to a definite quantity of force suggests conservation of energy, and an earlier note says "The principle of the conservation of energy demands *eternal recurrence*" (WP 1063, KSA 12:5[54]). The reference to a definite number of centers of force similarly suggests the conservation of matter. Nietzsche follows Boscovich in describing atoms, the constitutents of matter, this way (BGE 12). The conservation laws Nietzsche indicates forbid any accretion or dissipation of energy or gain or loss of matter that would prevent a return to previous states. These laws therefore favor reversibility.

Conservation laws are however insufficient to guarantee reversibility. The universe might for example be eternally expanding, as astronomical evidence after Nietzsche's time suggests. Poincaré's theorem assumes that phase space is restricted to measure-preserving transformations, an assumption refutable by further empirical evidence. Though Poincaré's proof states its assumptions more precisely than Nietzsche's note, neither applies to our universe if endless expansion permits infinite possible future states.

Next in this paragraph, Nietzsche indicates the second premise and draws the conclusion. He writes that "In infinite time, every possible combination would

---

[12] Small (2017) notes that Poincaré's theorem only has particles returning arbitrarily close to their initial conditions, not necessarily to their exact previous locations. A sufficiently close return regenerates the same supervening psychological and evaluative properties. Parfit (1984) regards personal identity and everything that matters as supervening on these psychological and evalu-ative properties. Nietzsche's determinism may still be better than Poincaré's indeterminism for preserving identity, as Section 8 discusses.

at some time or another be realized; more: it would be realized an infinite number of times." To fill infinite time, systems with no irreversible processes must repeat some of their states an infinite number of times. This reasoning is shared by both Nietzsche and Poincaré.

Additional assumptions allow Nietzsche to draw conclusions that Poincaré does not. Additionally assuming determinism entails a universe where events all recur eternally in identical cycles. Without determinism, this is conceivable but extremely improbable, requiring chance events to go the same way in every cycle an infinite number of times. Determinism leaves nothing to chance, as each event determines the next event. As Nietzsche concludes the paragraph:

> And since between every combination and its next recurrence all other possible combinations would have to take place, and each of these combinations conditions the entire sequence of combinations in the same series, a circular movement of absolutely identical series is thus demonstrated: the world as a circular movement that has already repeated itself infinitely often and plays its game *in infinitum*. (WP 1066 / KSA 11:38[12])

Determinism entails that each combination of matter and energy will condition the entire sequence, with the recurrence of any state initiating a new identical cycle. Identical states A_1 and A_2 at distinct times will respectively be succeeded by identical states B_1 and B_2, which themselves will respectively be succeeded by identical states C_1 and C_2, and so on. When a state Z_1 gives rise to A_2, B_2 will follow, and the cycles beginning with A_1 and A_2 will be identical.

Determinism reduces the probability of lives starting exactly like ours but proceeding differently. Differences that we can't detect may still allow some lives that begin just like ours in every detectable way but then take a different turn due to undetected factors. But determinism prevents lives that begin with the exact same state of the universe from going differently.

Poincaré's theorem lacks this deterministic assumption. It therefore allows identical states A_1 and A_2 at distinct times to respectively be succeeded by different states X and Y. While determinism organizes states into identical cycles of eternal recurrence, indeterminism shuffles states into the noncyclical and irregular repetitions of Poincaré's theorem.[13] So two identical states exactly like those beginning our lives need not continue into identical lives. But even assuming indeterminism, entire lives identical to ours may recur due to the sheer vastness of infinite time. These fully identical lives would be interspersed in time between a vast range of lives that start identically and proceed differently. There would also be lives that begin differently and have long identical sequences, and all sorts of other lives.

---

[13] Bocchieri and Loinger (1957) prove a quantum version of Poincaré's theorem.

Some have taken eternal recurrence to conflict with the second law of thermodynamics, which says that the entropy of the universe increases over time. According to the second law, ordered states suited for predictable and orderly discharges of energy give way to states where energy takes the disordered and unpredictable form of entropy. Ernst Zermelo (1896) interprets the second law as true without exception, entailing irreversible rising entropy. He therefore regards the second law as refuting Poincaré's theorem and the Newtonian-mechanical worldview suggesting it. Nietzsche was aware of similar reasoning proceeding from the second law. Just before the paragraph arguing for recurrence he writes, "If, e.g., the mechanistic theory cannot avoid the consequence, drawn for it by William Thomson, of leading to a final state, then the mechanistic theory stands refuted." Thomson (also called Lord Kelvin, and an early discoverer of the second law) took mechanistic theories to entail a high-entropy final state. Nietzsche therefore saw recurrence as potentially refuting mechanistic theories.

Ludwig Boltzmann's (1896) reply to Zermelo explains how mechanistic theories, recurrence, and the second law are jointly consistent. Boltzmann treats the second law as holding only in a probabilistic and path-dependent fashion which favors exceptions under some conditions. A high proportion of the possible states are chaotic and disordered, and initial conditions have in general been extremely well-ordered. So perturbing any system near initial conditions will likely increase disorder overall. However, an extremely disordered system would by similar randomness proceed toward order, and perhaps into highly ordered states after some time. Brush quotes Poincaré's remark that "to see heat pass from a cold body to a warm one, it will not be necessary to have the acute vision, the intelligence, and the dexterity of Maxwell's demon; it will suffice to have a little patience" (632).

Thinking the eternal recurrence refuted mechanistic theories, Nietzsche favored a nonmechanistic alternative using the will to power to ground Boscovich's conception of atoms as centers of force.[14] Here Thomson's absolute conception of the second law of thermodynamics, shared by Zermelo, seems to have led Nietzsche wrong. Boltzmann's probabilistic account of the second law renders mechanistic theories consistent with eternal recurrence, leaving no problem for will to power to solve.

For systems as vast as the universe, the progress from disorder to order required for Poincaré recurrence is extremely slow. Don Page (1994) estimates the Poincaré recurrence time for something with the mass of the whole universe

---

[14] KSA 11:38[12] emphasizes this view. See Poellner (1995), Whitlock (1997), and Ansell-Pearson (2000) for discussion. Nolt (2008) argues that the eternal recurrence is independent of the will to power. Löwith (1997) regards these doctrines as incompatible.

at around $10^\wedge 10^\wedge 10^\wedge 4$ trillion days. A number extending from the earth to the moon where every digit is a typed 9 would be far less than this number of days. Page doesn't actually specify units for this calculation, noting that the error bars on this estimate are so vast that switching the units from days to milliseconds or millennia is swamped by other uncertainties.

There is however no clear way for the unthinkable vastness of the time between repetitions of states to prevent recurrence. If time continues infinitely into the future, even this incomprehensibly vast period will elapse infinite times, and all our lives will recur eternally. Infinity is that big! Of course, any irreversible processes that haven't made their presence felt in the 14 billion years since the Big Bang might do so over the additional vast time Page describes, preventing recurrence. But then an irreversible process prevents recurrence, not the mere length of the recurrence time. Eternity contains infinite repetitions of even the vast recurrence times Page suggests.

Because of subsequently discovered irreversible processes like cosmic expansion which indicate an infinite phase space, our universe seems not to satisfy Nietzsche and Poincaré's assumptions. Contemporary scientific evidence counts against the universe eternally recurring as they imagined. But reality might still contain a vast number of duplicates or near-duplicates of ourselves.[15] If reality is big enough and Earth-like conditions are probable enough, many people might have lives indistinguishable from ours somewhere at some time. Whether they stand in any ethically interesting relation to us is an interesting question. Even if they aren't extensions of us in the way that ourselves in future cycles of recurrence are, perhaps we should feel some closeness to them. We have after all been through the same things. Moreover, faraway beings who are aware of the vastness of reality might think about us, just as this sentence expresses a thought about them. Under the right conditions, they could love us, and we could love them back.[16] Nietzsche's thoughts about the eternal recurrence are an advance in human thought about relations to beings far from here and now.

Views in Nietzsche's unpublished notes cannot generally be treated as his firm and settled conclusions. Pietro Gori (2019) observes that "Nietzsche's notebooks contain draft observations which, consequently, can only be considered as steps of a still developing reflection" and criticizes interpreters who "ascribe to the fragments the same value they attribute to a published text" (43 n3). If the published works are like the answers a student turns in on a math test, the unpublished notes are like scrap paper with calculations that the student may

---

[15] Lewis (1986) argues for a metaphysical multiverse; Greene (2011) discusses multiverse theories in physics.

[16] Sinhababu (2008).

have ultimately rejected. The unpublished notes show that Nietzsche considered a particular idea or argument, but they don't show that he remained confident in it. He might become confident of an idea in the notes and publish it or something similar, but he also might abandon it or regard his earlier phrasing as misleading. While the will to power is developed considerably in the unpublished notes, it makes less of an appearance in the published works, where it doesn't take a definite or consistent form. That is part of why I don't emphasize it here, except to note its connection to the rejection of atomism, for which it may not even be necessary.[17]

While KSA 11:38[12] shows that Nietzsche considered something close to Poincare's argument, he never published anything similarly explicit and straightforward. *Zarathustra* presents the argument in visions and poetic statements by fictional characters, and doesn't confidently present it as a truth about our world. Nietzsche's detailed understanding of the argument likely made him aware that not all premises were certain. Perhaps he recognized that he couldn't defend assumptions like the absence of very slow irreversible processes. But he saw no clear refutation of these assumptions. He moreover understood that infinity was vast enough to ensure eternal recurrence even with the longest finite recurrence times. This made him hopeful but uncertain about the eternal recurrence.

KSA 11:38[12] is good evidence that the eternal recurrence was important to Nietzsche until the end of his career. References to the eternal recurrence in the published works after *Zarathustra* further demonstrate this. *Beyond Good and Evil* describes the eternal recurrence as "the ideal of the most high-spirited, alive, and world-affirming human being who has not only come to terms and learned to get along with whatever was and is, but who wants to have *what was and is* repeated into all eternity, shouting insatiably *da capo*" (BGE 56). While the eternal recurrence is absent from many subsequent works including *The Antichrist*, the *Genealogy*, and *The Case of Wagner*, it re-emerges in *Twilight of the Idols*. This book ends with Nietzsche describing himself as "the teacher of the eternal recurrence" (TI "Ancients" 5), followed by a concluding passage from *Zarathustra* titled "The Hammer Speaks." Thomas Brobjer (2023) recognizes that Nietzsche symbolically connects hammers to the eternal recurrence in the unpublished notes, making this a further sign of the continued significance of the idea. Nietzsche's final work *Ecce Homo* also ascribes great significance to the eternal recurrence, as noted at the beginning of this Element.

---

[17] Nietzsche presents the will to power as a fundamental ontology underlying physics in BGE 22, but then seems to concede that it is "only an interpretation."

Nietzsche planned to write more about the eternal recurrence. Brobjer shows that from 1881 to 1885 he planned a book called "The Recurrence of the Same" [*Die Wiederkunft des Gleichen*] or "The Eternal Recurrence" [*Die ewige Wiederkunft*]. In 1885, plans for this book merged into plans for a masterwork first titled *The Will to Power* and finally *Revaluation of all Values*. This masterwork would defend recurrence as a cosmological thesis, and discuss how different people would respond to the cosmology by becoming more nihilistic or more life-affirming. Perhaps Nietzsche had come to fully accept the argument of KSA 11:38[12], and planned to state it in his own voice rather than a hypothetical or fictional voice.

We will never know what Nietzsche would have written if fate granted him a few more years, or even a few more weeks. Perhaps his doubts would have returned in comprehensively articulating the argument, when problems arose in defending its underlying assumptions. We can only imagine what he might have written if he had learned of Poincaré's theorem.

Nietzsche's actual thoughts about eternal recurrence are best expressed in his favorite actual book, which contains vivid symbolic illustrations of the cosmology of recurrence. It tells of a philosopher falling in love with Eternity. We now turn to this science fiction love story, *Thus Spoke Zarathustra*.

4 "The Soothsayer" Envisions the Dark Side of Eternal Recurrence

The story of the eternal recurrence in *Zarathustra* begins with a soothsayer's prophecy illustrating the bad consequences of accepting it. This prophecy makes Zarathustra have a dream about the long lifeless period in a cycle of recurrence. Though he doesn't fully understand the prophecy or the dream, they provide his first glimpses of the eternal recurrence, which he gradually comes to accept, understand, and teach over the rest of the Element.

Foreshadowing from the previous section suggests that an important idea will soon emerge. A mysterious follower called Zarathustra's shadow flies through the air toward a volcanic island and calling out "It is time! It is high time!" Zarathustra himself is exploring the volcano to argue with a fire hound about how the course of history is determined.[18] While the fire hound thinks political upheavals drive history, Zarathustra tells him that history revolves around the "inventors of new values," and that the greatest events "are not our loudest but our stillest hours." After emerging from the volcano, Zarathustra learns what his shadow said, and the section ends as he wonders "High time for *what?*" (Z II:

---

[18] The fire hound seems to represent the English historian Henry Thomas Buckle, whom GM I:4 associates with volcanos and describes in similar terms.

"On Great Events"). It is high time for Zarathustra's first vision of the eternal recurrence, about which his stillest hour will speak to him.

"The Soothsayer" begins with a dark prophecy from its eponymous character: "–And I saw a great sadness descend upon mankind. The best grew weary of their works. A doctrine appeared, accompanied by a faith: 'All is empty, all is the same, all has been!' And from all the hills it echoed: 'All is empty, all is the same, all has been.'" The soothsayer prophesies a future where people accept the eternal recurrence, viewing their own lives as a repetition of past events, and are dismayed because they see life as pointlessly bad.[19] They wish to die forever and be freed from the meaninglessness of existence, but the eternal recurrence allows no such escape. Annihilating oneself eternally is impossible, as whatever one lives of one's life will eternally return.[20] The prophecy concludes with their anguish at being unable to end their existence: "'Alas, where is there still a sea in which one might drown?' thus are we wailing across shallow swamps. Verily, we have become too weary even to die. We are still waking and living on – in tombs" (Z II: "The Soothsayer"). Those who know they will simply relive the dreary and pointless life of their now-dead past selves might find living in tombs a natural metaphor for their existence.

The soothsayer's gloomy prophecy depresses Zarathustra. Worried that "this long twilight will come," he doesn't eat for three days and stops speaking to anyone. He then falls asleep and envisions the cosmology of the eternal recurrence in a symbolic dream.

In Zarathustra's dream, he "had turned his back on all life" and become a "night watchman and a guardian of tombs upon the lonely mountain castle of death." The tombs contain "Life that had been overcome," and the castle has the "odor of dusty eternities" (Z II: "The Soothsayer"). Zarathustra is viewing life as it will be for the utterly vast lengths of time during which everyone has died, and before the cycle of recurrence brings everyone back again. In this sense he is the night watchman over the eons when the light of life goes out in the universe, until its brief return.

Befitting a night watchman Zarathustra has the keys to the gate of the castle of death. When he tries to open it, his efforts result only in a loud and unpleasant noise, after which an even more unpleasant "death-rattle silence" returns. References to death are appropriately omnipresent in this dream, as it represents the period when nobody exists and all are dead, waiting to be reborn. The dream again represents the incomprehensible vastness of this period: "Thus time

---

[19] Gooding-Williams (2001) likens the soothsayer's views to Schopenhauer's pessimism. Janaway (2022) distinguishes them.

[20] Nietzsche may not have initially recognized this in (KSA 9:11[141]).

passed and crawled, if time still existed – how should I know?" (Z II: "The Soothsayer"). Here we might recall Don Page's estimate of how long recurrence would take for something with the mass of the universe – approximately ten to the power of ten to the power of a number with four trillion digits.

Eventually the gate opens not because of his efforts, but because of a natural force – a "roaring wind." (Z II: "The Soothsayer"). The cosmology of eternal recurrence includes vast periods without human beings, and presumably without other intelligent life. So it requires natural forces rather than intentional action to explain the return of life-supporting conditions and life itself. In keeping with Nietzsche's early notes rejecting the idea of the universe as striving toward a goal (KSA 9:11[157]) or as an organism (KSA 9:11[201]), an inanimate force brings about eternal recurrence.

The roaring wind breaks open one of the coffins containing life that had been overcome. This symbolic freeing of life from death represents the return of living beings to the cosmos in the cycle of recurrence. What emerges from the coffin has all the variety and chaotic energy of life. Zarathustra hears "a thousandfold laughter," and witnesses "a thousand grimaces of children, angels, owls, fools, and butterflies as big as children" (Z II: "The Soothsayer"). He cries out in horror and wakes up.

After waking, Zarathustra explains the dream to his disciples, asking them to help him "guess its meaning," and saying "This dream is still a riddle to me." His favorite disciple interprets the dream as representing Zarathustra's victory over his enemies. This interpretation identifies Zarathustra with "the wind with the shrill whistling that tears open the gates of the castles of death," and the "coffin full of colorful sarcasms and the angelic grimaces of life." There is some textual evidence for the disciple's interpretation, as Zarathustra sometimes metaphorically identifies himself with the wind while giving speeches on the blessed isles. But the interpretation makes poor sense of Zarathustra's position within the dream itself. Zarathustra is the night watchman rather than the wind, which succeeds in opening the gate where he fails. Zarathustra moreover can't be identified with the contents of the coffin, as he views it from outside, and its contents surprise and frighten him. The disciple moreover identifies his enemies as "all the night watchmen and guardians of tombs and at whoever else is rattling with gloomy keys" (Z II: "The Soothsayer"). But the night watchman is Zarathustra, not an enemy. The wind moreover opens the gate, which the night watchman tried to do, leaving little reason for enmity between them.

Rather than accepting his disciples' triumphalist interpretation, Zarathustra sits silently for a long time until they lift him to his feet. Upon rising, he suggests that they all eat together and feed the soothsayer too. The phrase "Thus spoke Zarathustra" then appears, but rather than ending the section as usual, it is followed by "But then he looked a long time into the face of the disciple who had played the dream interpreter and he shook his head." Zarathustra realizes that the disciple's interpretation of the dream is mistaken.

Less obviously, this realization appears after "Thus spoke Zarathustra" to indicate that there is something he can't say – namely, that the disciple is wrong because the dream is really about the eternal recurrence (Z II: "The Soothsayer"). This is his first vision of recurrence, seen from the perspective of the vast eons for which no life exists, until natural forces align in a way that brings life back again. But lacking explicit understanding of his dream, he is unable to say what he dreamt of.

From this section onward, the central drama of *Zarathustra* concerns the eternal recurrence. The difficulty of interpreting the unclear prophecy and the symbolic dream leads many scholars not to see them as envisioning the eternal recurrence.[21] But a close look at both visions as well as the foreshadowing in "On Great Events" supports Robert Gooding-Williams' (2001) view that this section discusses the eternal recurrence, and especially Lawrence Hatab's (2005) view that Zarathustra's engagement with it begins here.

Later sections point back to "The Soothsayer" as describing the first appearance of the eternal recurrence in Zarathustra's mind. The next section, "On Redemption," describes how the idea proceeds further into his explicit and conscious thought. Later Zarathustra describes "the wanderer's shadow," the "longest boredom" (apparently the great weariness of the soothsayer's prophecy), and the "stillest hour" as signs that "It is high time" for the idea of eternal recurrence, which he didn't recognize until his "abysmal thought" bit him (Z III: "On Involuntary Bliss"). The soothsayer is his main antagonist in the philosophical struggle that unfolds over the course of Part IV, which ends with Zarathustra's triumph as they welcome the eternal recurrence together. All this makes full dramatic sense if the soothsayer's prophecy and the resulting dream are the emergence of the idea of recurrence into Zarathustra's mind.

5 "On Redemption" Tells of the Will's Struggle with the Past

Zarathustra's next speech discusses how bad past events frustrate the will, and how the will can redeem the past from them. His interlocutor in this section is a wise hunchback who makes the self-deprecating joke that he has "too much behind him," and asks Zarathustra to "take away a little." This is a metaphor for how bad past events burden us, and how we would like them not to have been. This would of course change the character of the present, making us otherwise

---

[21] Lampert (1986), Rosen (1995), Seung (2005), Loeb (2010), and Burnham and Jesinghausen (2010).

than we now are. Zarathustra accordingly declines the hunchback's request, saying "When one takes away the hump from the hunchback one takes away his spirit" (Z II: "On Redemption").

Zarathustra tells the hunchback that what bothers him most about the past is the wretchedness of the misshapen people in it. Noting that he isn't so troubled by literal disability, he discusses the flawed character even of those regarded as the greatest human beings, who often have one impressive ability but otherwise worthless character. His memorable example is someone whose body was mostly a "tremendous ear" that gave him amazing abilities, but who otherwise had little more than a "tiny envious face" and a "bloated little soul."[22] More generally, he describes finding "man in ruins and scattered as over a battlefield or a butcher-field. And when my eyes flee from the now to the past, they always find the same: fragments and limbs and dreadful accidents – but no human beings" (Z II: "On Redemption").

Any plausible account of value will find many horrible things in the past. The worst things in human history might include famines, genocides, wars, and long eras of brutal oppression. If the millions of years before humans include much more animal suffering than animal happiness, Earth may be more a hell than a heaven for its sentient inhabitants over the entirety of its existence. Even if Zarathustra's focus on the wretchedness of human character is distinctive to his own evaluative outlook, other views will find much to agree with in his account of how the horrible past frustrates the will:

> "It was" – that is the name of the will's gnashing of teeth and most secret melancholy. Powerless against what has been done, he is an angry spectator of all that is past. The will cannot will backwards; and that he cannot break time and time's covetousness, that is the will's loneliest melancholy. (Z II: "On Redemption")

Nothing can be done to change past events, as action affects only the future. Many good people died brutal deaths at the hands of genocidal killers; countless baby animals found no food and knew nothing of life but starvation. Any heroic will to save these unfortunate beings is thwarted by time itself. As Lawrence Hatab (2005) begins by noting, any adult life will have its share of tragedy and regret. Past tragedy can't be averted; regretted action can't be undone.

Zarathustra recognizes that the unchangeable nature of the past confounds his emphasis of creative and passionate acts of will. He recognizes this, saying "Will – that is the name of the liberator and joy-bringer; thus I taught you, my friends. But now learn this too: the will itself is still a prisoner." While bad future events can sometimes be averted through acts of will, especially with

---

[22] This seems to be Richard Wagner, with his musical talent represented by the ear.

creativity and passion, there is no changing the past. This leaves even the most creative and passionate will an "angry spectator" regarding bad past events. Zarathustra describes the frustrated will as seeking revenge against time and the past, as if against a person. He clarifies what he means by revenge: "This, indeed this alone, is what *revenge* is: the will's ill will against time and its 'it was.'" Then he describes the frustrated will looking upon time and the past with a "*spirit of revenge*" (Z II: "On Redemption").

The spirit of revenge treats time itself as a wrongdoer who must be punished. Revenge is standardly a response to the deeds of persons rather than inanimate entities. Revenge against time accordingly requires treating time as if it were a person. The psychological drive toward this conception of time comes from suffering, as "where there was suffering, one always wanted punishment too." A vengeful will can flatter itself as rightfully punishing the past, "For 'punishment' is what revenge calls itself; with a hypocritical lie it creates a good conscience for itself" (Z II: "On Redemption"). Earlier, Zarathustra lamented the worldview generated by this desire to punish: "Alas, that is my sorrow: they have lied reward and punishment into the foundation of things, and now also into the foundation of your souls, you who are virtuous" (Z II: "On the Virtuous"). He then said "*that man be delivered from revenge*, that is for me the bridge to the highest hope, and a rainbow after long storms" (Z II: "On the Tarantulas").[23] As Zarathustra only metaphorically describes the revenge the will might take against the past, it may be useful to consider a more explicit account that Nietzsche offered years later.

The first essay of the *Genealogy* describes how early Christians' desire for revenge against their pagan enemies generated their conceptions of the afterlife, free will, and morality. Unable to avenge themselves against their politically powerful enemies, they fantasized about an afterlife where God damns the pagans to eternal torment as a just punishment for doing evil of their own free will. Wishful thinking turned this revenge fantasy into their view of the afterlife. Nietzsche quotes Thomas Aquinas' remark that "In order that the bliss of the saints may be more delightful for them and that they may render more copious thanks to God for it, it is given to them to see perfectly the punishment of the damned" (GM I:15 49 fn.1).

Nietzsche's extended quotation from the second century writer Tertullian, sometimes described as "the father of Latin Christianity" and the "founder of Western theology," vividly illustrates the spirit of revenge.[24] Discussing Jesus' return and the final judgment, he says "But think of what awaits us on the day of his return, the day of his triumph!" (GM I:15, note 1, 49). He eagerly anticipates

---

[23] Noted by Drochon (2016).   [24] Benham (1887), Ekonomou (2007), and Gonzalez (2010).

witnessing the incineration of the pagans in hell – actors "in the dissolving flame," wrestlers "tossing in the fiery billows," and philosophers "covered with shame before the poor deluded ones, as one fire consumes them!" (GM I:15, note 2, 49–50). Nietzsche writes that Tertullian "has conceived 'the evil enemy,' '*the Evil One*,' and this in fact is his basic concept, from which he then evolves, as an afterthought and pendant, a 'good one' – himself!" (GM I:10, 39). Since pagan values aligned with strong passions that all humans share for things like physical pleasures, Christians are left with values formed in opposition to such passions. Nietzsche contends that these values have left Christians with an internally divided and self-frustrating psychology ever since.

The spirit of revenge leads the will to four teachings of madness. First is the view that all mortal and timebound things deserve their mortality, which Nietzsche finds in Anaximander: "'Everything passes away; therefore everything deserves to pass away. And this too is justice, this law of time that it must devour its children.'[25] Thus preached madness." Second is a cosmology of punishment coming from Schopenhauer: "'Things are ordered morally according to justice and punishment.[26] Alas, where is redemption from the flux of things and from the punishment called existence?' Thus preached madness." Third is Tertullian's hell itself: "'Can there be redemption if there is eternal justice? Alas, the stone *It was* cannot be moved: all punishments must be eternal too.' Thus preached madness." Fourth is: "No deed can be annihilated: how could it be undone by punishment? This, this is what is eternal in the punishment called existence, that existence must eternally become deed and guilt again." Zarathustra continues, "But, my brothers, you know this fable of madness," perhaps indicating that it concerns a familiar real-world doctrine like original sin (Z II: "On Redemption").

Zarathustra's discussion of the spirit of revenge reaches its climax as he describes how the will could escape its teachings of madness by willing the past. This would happen when "the creative will says to it, 'But thus I will it; thus shall I will it.'" Such an embrace of the past would be the will's "reconciliation with time and something higher than any reconciliation." The question is, "how shall this be brought about? Who could teach him also to will backwards?" (Z II: "On Redemption").

Immediately after saying that, Zarathustra "suddenly stopped and looked altogether like one who has received a severe shock" (Z II: "On Redemption"). This is the shock of his first explicit thought of the eternal recurrence. The soothsayer's prophecy and his ensuing dream planted the seeds of the idea. Now he seeks a way to overcome the spirit of revenge and reconcile the will

---

[25] Shapiro (2016).   [26] Janaway (2022).

with the past, and discovers that willing the eternal recurrence would do it. This would be willing backward, as one wills all times including the past to recur.

The past would be redeemed if we could will it exactly as it was, as Paul Loeb (2010) emphasizes, and this is part of willing the eternal recurrence.[27] But if the past is so horrible that it leaves the will possessed by a spirit of revenge against time itself, how could it be willed to exist for eternity? Zarathustra's horror is specifically about the eternal recurrence of contemptible people, but every plausible view of value will see much of the past as horrific. The eternal recurrence threatens to turn the finite horrors of the past into infinite horror, and how could anyone will that? As Zarathustra encounters the idea of the eternal recurrence in connection with negative value rather than positive value, he regards it with horror rather joy, and finds it literally unspeakable.

As in "The Soothsayer," the words "Thus spoke Zarathustra" don't end the section, again indicating that there is something Zarathustra can't say (Z II: "On Redemption"). Previously he was silent despite knowing that his disciple's interpretation of his dream was wrong, perhaps because he didn't have a better interpretation to offer. He hadn't understood the cosmology in his dreams and how it might fulfill the soothsayer's dark prophecy. Now he sees its infinite horror.

This time "Thus spoke Zarathustra" is followed by two perceptive questions from the hunchback, who recognizes that Zarathustra is holding something back. The first is "But why does Zarathustra speak otherwise to us than to his disciples?" Zarathustra's reply is evasive: "What is surprising in that? With hunchbacks one may well speak in a hunchbacked way." The perceptive hunchback follows up, "All right ... and one may well tell pupils tales out of school. But why does Zarathustra speak otherwise to his pupils than to him-self?" (Z II: "On Redemption").

The answer is that Zarathustra can't bring himself to speak of the infinite horror unleashed by the eternal recurrence. To say this would be speak of it. So there is nothing he can say.

6 "The Stillest Hour" Struggles to Speak of Infinite Negative Value

The next three sections describe Zarathustra's emotional struggle with the idea of the eternal recurrence, and especially with the infinite depths of negative value that it generates. This is particularly a focus of the second section, "The Stillest Hour."

---

[27] Loeb notes that Heidegger (1991), Pippin (1988), Berkowitz (1995), and Gooding-Williams (2001) think Nietzsche's conception of redemption requires changing the past. All but Gooding-Williams treat this as rendering it impossible.

"On Human Prudence" begins by describing how infinities of value affect our emotions, using metaphors of elevation familiar to mountain climbers: "Not the height but the precipice is terrible. That precipice where the glance plunges *down* and the hand reaches *up*. There the heart becomes giddy confronted with its double will." Here, the emotions of engaging with infinities of value are compared to fear of heights when looking into a precipice. These infinities extend in both directions, as Zarathustra expresses by asking, "Alas, friends, can you guess what is my heart's double will?" (Z II: "On Human Prudence"). Unable to speak clearly of infinite negative value, he leaves his friends to guess. He then discusses the heights and depths of his value theory, the greatness of the superhuman and the contemptible state of contemporary man – a familiar theme from the *Prologue*.[28] Most of the section describes Zarathustra's four strategies for coping with the smallness of humanity – not guarding against deception, sparing the vain, appreciating great evildoers, and misjudging everyone. His emotional turmoil suggests that these coping mechanisms are insufficient to deal with thoughts of infinite negative value.

"The Stillest Hour" describes Zarathustra's internal conflict about whether to proclaim the eternal recurrence. He recounts this conversation in explaining to his followers why he must leave them: "Alas, my angry mistress wants it, she spoke to me; have I ever yet mentioned her name to you? Yesterday, toward evening, there spoke to me *my stillest hour*: that is the name of my awesome mistress" (Z II: "The Stillest Hour"). Zarathustra previously used these words for the quiet moments when world-changing ideas occur to us, during his debate with the fire hound in "On Great Events." There it foreshadowed the emergence of the eternal recurrence in Zarathustra's mind. Here the stillest hour is personified, and commands Zarathustra to overcome his reluctance and publicly proclaim the eternal recurrence.

Zarathustra's conversation with his stillest hour reveals his awareness of the eternal recurrence, as well as his inability to proclaim it. She tells him, "You know it, Zarathustra, but you do not say it!" He replies, "Yes, I know it, but I do not want to say it!" His reluctance surprises her. When he says, "Alas, I would like to, but how can I? Let me off from this! It is beyond my strength!" she commands him to "Speak your word and break!" He then makes the excuse that nobody listens to him – "As yet my words have not moved mountains, and what I said did not reach men" – and that he lacks the "lion's voice for commanding." She rejects his excuses by noting that world-changing ideas often have little immediate effect on the world, just as he previously told the fire hound: "It is the

---

[28] I use Kaufmann's translation of *Zarathustra* and other books when possible for consistency. However, I render *Übermensch* as "superhuman," which expresses some of the original term's meaning and preserves the gender-neutrality of *-mensch*. See Loeb and Tinsley (2022).

stillest words that bring on the storm. Thoughts that come on doves' feet guide the world." Lacking any good response, he finally says, "I am ashamed" (Z II: "The Stillest Hour").

The stillest hour's final reply diagnoses his problem and prescribes a solution: "your fruit is ripe, but you are not ripe for your fruit. Thus you must return to your solitude again; for you must yet become mellow" (Z II: "The Stillest Hour"). As Mark Alfano (2019) describes, Nietzsche treats solitude as a virtue because it allows for fuller development of one's own distinctive ideas.[29] The disciple's flattering but incorrect interpretation of the dream in "On the Vision and the Riddle" indicates how the company of others can interfere with this. The stillest hour tells Zarathustra to seek solitude so that he can fully process and develop the idea of eternal recurrence.

Though Zarathustra is sad to leave his friends, he follows the stillest hour's command and begins a long journey back to his cave. "The Wanderer" begins after he parts from his disciples to journey on alone. The events from "The Soothsayer" forward have been set in the blessed isles (which are near the volcanic island of "On Great Events"). Now he plans his departure from the region, and crosses the mountainous ridge of the island to board a ship that will take him homeward.

In these mountains between the seas, he considers how great heights and depths of value are joined together, returning to metaphors of elevation: "Whence come the highest mountains? I once asked. Then I learned that they came out of the sea. The evidence is written in their rocks and in the walls of their peaks. It is out of the deepest depth that the highest must come to its height" (Z III: "The Wanderer"). He is not yet ready to will an eternal journey through these depths and heights.

Zarathustra has distinctive views about the depths and heights of value. The depths of value consist in the existence of contemptible and disgusting people. This is why the misshapen human beings he describes in "On Redemption" trouble him so much. He places great value on great human individuals. This is why "On Human Prudence" discusses the possibility of creating the super-human at such length.

Those with different views about the depths and heights of value might have equally strong feelings about the eternal recurrence. Those horrified by the lifelong misery of oppressed or impoverished people might be overwhelmed with horror at thinking of their reliving their suffering an infinite number of times for eternity. They are in an eternal hell, which they did nothing to deserve. For others who are luckier, the eternal recurrence will be an eternal heaven. If

---

[29] Remhof (2018) discusses the "loneliness" in which the demon of GS 341 speaks.

humanity overcomes the dangers and troubles of the present age and emerges into a long and happy future, there will be eternities of joy for our blessed descendants. Even if we accept a very different value theory than Zarathustra, the eternal recurrence might give our hearts a similar double will.

Many wonder how Nietzsche can reject morality while making forceful value judgments himself. I join those who think he regards all moral belief as false because there are no moral facts, while believing in subjective value that lacks the objectivity and universality of morality.[30] Aesthetic value is often understood as subjective in this way – beauty is in the eye of the beholder. The heights of value Zarathustra sees in the superhuman and the depths of value he sees in those he despises can be subjective, like beauty and ugliness.

To a confident believer in objective moral value, it might seem strange to be so concerned about subjective value. But if there is no objective value of any kind, subjective value is all we have.[31] Zarathustra faces the possibility of infinitely long existence in a world of unredeemed ugliness. This infinite negative value what he finds unspeakable.

7 "On the Vision and the Riddle" Envisions the Cosmology

Zarathustra then boards a ship taking him away from the Blessed Isles. There is "much that was strange and dangerous to be heard" aboard the ship, "which came from far away and wanted to sail even farther." This adventuresome environment inspires Zarathustra articulate the eternal recurrence more explicitly than before, after remaining silent for two days at sea. He tells the "bold searchers, researchers, and whoever embarks with cunning sails on terrible seas" of "the riddle that I saw, the vision of the loneliest" (Z III: "Vision and Riddle").

In Zarathustra's vision, he is climbing a mountain while carrying a dwarf whom he calls the "spirit of gravity, my devil and archenemy," and who draws him "downward towards the abyss." The dwarf taunts Zarathustra in addition to physically impeding his upward progress, saying "You threw yourself up high, but every stone that is thrown must fall" (Z III: "Vision and Riddle"). True to his name, this spirit of gravity is literally and metaphorically trying to bring Zarathustra down. Here again elevation symbolizes value. The downward force exerted by the spirit of gravity recalls how the eternal recurrence was first presented in GS 341, as "The greatest weight."

Summoning up his courage to challenge his enemy, Zarathustra says "Dwarf! It is you or I!" He describes how courage "slays dizziness at the edge of

---

[30] Langsam (1997), Robertson (2012), and Sinhababu (2015).
[31] Williams (forthcoming) defends such a view.

abysses" and "slays even pity," which he calls "the deepest abyss." The abysses represent negative value, with pity being a response to negative value in the lives of others. Eternal repetition gives these abysses infinite depth. Courage slays dizziness at the depths of abysses in enabling mental engagement with infinite negative value. Zarathustra then considers how courage might lead him to wish for life to recur. He praises "courage which attacks: which slays even death itself, for it says, 'Was that life? Well then! Once more!'" (Z III: "Vision and Riddle"). Strictly speaking, he doesn't accept the eternal recurrence here, both because he wishes only for one additional episode of life, and because he praises the sort of courage that would lead him to endorse it rather than actually endorsing it himself. But it is the closest he has come.

Zarathustra tells the dwarf, "you do not know my abysmal thought. *That* you could not bear!" Then "something happened that made me lighter, for the dwarf jumped from my shoulder, being curious" (Z III: "Vision and Riddle"). Zarathustra's abysmal thought is later revealed as being that "The small man recurs eternally!" (Z III: "The Convalescent"). The dwarf, whom Loeb (2010) recognizes as a literal small man, will weigh on Zarathustra less as he comes closer to accepting the eternal recurrence. The dwarf jumps off Zarathustra's shoulder as he exercises the level of courage needed to speak of his "abysmal thought" [*abgründlichen Gedanken*]. This the thought that weighs Zarathustra down, making him look deep into abysses [*Abgründen*] of value. (Z III: "Vision and Riddle").

In front of them is a gateway. As Zarathustra describes it, "Two paths meet here; no one has yet followed either to its end. This long lane stretches back for an eternity. And the long lane out there, that is another eternity." He asks, "do you believe, dwarf, that these paths contradict each other eternally?" The dwarf replies "contemptuously," "'All that is straight lies . . . All truth is crooked; time itself is a circle.'" Zarathustra responds angrily, not to contradict the dwarf, but to tell him "You spirit of gravity . . . do not make things too easy for yourself!" (Z III: "Vision and Riddle").

Zarathustra's point is that the dwarf won't succeed in depressing him. As Loeb (2010) argues, he isn't saying that the dwarf is wrong about the circular structure of time.[32] As the spirit of gravity, the dwarf's aim is to bring Zarathustra down with thoughts of the infinite negative value introduced by the eternal recurrence. He may be doing the same with his repeated message of how thrown stones must fall, alluding to the conservation of matter and energy as Nietzsche does in the unpublished notes. This suggests a finite phase space, favoring recurrence, as the argument of KSA 11:38[12] and Poincaré's theorem suggest.

---

[32] Loeb moreover points out that the two paths may indeed join far away and make a circle.

Zarathustra then describes the cosmology of eternal recurrence for the first time:

> From this gateway, Moment, a long, eternal lane leads *backward*: behind us lies an eternity. Must not whatever *can* walk have walked on this lane before? Must not whatever *can* happen have happened, have been done, have passed by before? And if everything has been there before – what do you think, dwarf, of this moment? Must not this gateway too have been there before? And are not all things knotted together so firmly that this moment draws after it all that is to come? Therefore itself too? For whatever can walk in this long lane out there too, it must walk once more. (Z III: "Vision and Riddle")

If time extends infinitely into both the past and the future, and if filling this infinity of time requires arrangements of matter like the present one to be repeated, there will be moments identical to the present in both directions. If such a universe proceeds according to deterministic laws that specify a unique series of events to follow any event, moments identical to the present will be followed by an identical sequence of events, until the present recurs again. When a moment like the present is reached, the cycle will begin again, leading back to itself over and over for eternity. Speaking more and more softly as he goes through this reasoning, Zarathustra draws the conclusion: "must we not eternally return?" (Z III: "Vision and Riddle").

As Zarathustra whispers of the eternal recurrence, he hears a dog howl and his dream shifts. The dwarf vanishes, never to be seen again. Zarathustra is transported to a nighttime scene with a young shepherd lying on the ground, "writhing, gagging, in spasms, his face distorted, and a heavy black snake hung out of his mouth." Beside him, the dog is howling to cry for help. Zarathustra tells the shepherd, "Bite! Bite its head off! Bite!"[33] (Z III: "Vision and Riddle").

The shepherd bites off the head of the snake, spits it out, jumps to his feet, and undergoes a miraculous transformation. He becomes "No longer shepherd, no longer human – one changed, radiant, laughing! Never yet on earth has a human being laughed as he laughed!" Again noting that this was "no human laughter," Zarathustra ends the section saying, "My longing for this laughter gnaws at me; oh, how do I bear to go on living! And how could I bear to die now!" (Z III: "Vision and Riddle").

Before this vision concludes, Zarathustra asks,

> You who are glad of riddles! Guess me this riddle that I saw then, interpret me the vision of the loneliest. For it was a vision and a foreseeing. *What* did I see

---

[33] Loeb notes that this section alludes to Act II of Wagner's *Ring* cycle, where the hero Siegfried kills a monstrous serpent and a malevolent dwarf. Siegfried then gains the ability to talk to birds (as Zarathustra will talk to his animals) and proposes marriage to his love (as Zarathustra will propose marriage to Eternity).

then in a parable? And *who* is it who must yet come one day? *Who* is the shepherd into whose throat the snake crawled thus? *Who* is the man into whose throat all that is heaviest and blackest will crawl thus?" (Z III: "Vision and Riddle").

Though Zarathustra again addresses this question to "searchers, researchers, and whoever among you has embarked with cunning sails on unexplored seas," the text includes no answers from his shipmates (Z III: "Vision and Riddle"). We readers are the audience he addresses, and his questions are ours to answer. The last two questions are largely equivalent, and have clear answers in the "The Convalescent." So the four questions are best answered in reverse order.

The shepherd is Zarathustra, answering the last two questions. He explains later that the snake represents his disgust with human wretchedness, especially if humanity recurs eternally:

> The great disgust with *man* – *this* choked me and had crawled into my throat; and what the soothsayer said: 'All is the same, nothing is worthwhile, knowledge chokes.' A long twilight limped before me, a sadness, weary to death, drunken with death, speaking with a yawning mouth. 'Eternally recurs the man of whom you are weary, the small man' – thus yawned my sadness and dragged its feet and could not go to sleep. (Z III: "The Convalescent").

The eternal recurrence is so hard for Zarathustra to accept because it entails that the most contemptible and wearying people will eternally return.

The one who must yet come one day is the superhuman, the inhuman being into whom the shepherd transforms. Although Zarathustra is the shepherd, this doesn't mean that he will become the superhuman. The shepherd undergoes such a radical transition, becoming someone who isn't a shepherd and isn't human, that his symbolic identity with Zarathustra can't be assumed to continue. The superhuman fits this description well, often being contrasted to the human. As there is little evidence that Zarathustra will become the superhuman or stop being human, he and the inhuman non-shepherd are best regarded as two different beings. Zarathustra's animals later mention that he will "proclaim the superhuman again to men" whenever he recurs (Z III: "The Convalescent"). This attests to the significance of the superhuman throughout the text. It also suggests that Zarathustra won't become the superhuman – otherwise, the animals would have more to say.

This returns us to Zarathustra's first question – what did he see? He saw the cosmological foundations of the eternal recurrence, how his contempt for the wretchedness of humanity is preventing him from accepting it, and how he might overcome this contempt. If humanity progresses far beyond its contemptible state and transforms into the superhuman, the present cycle will have positive value overall. The infinite repetitions of the eternal recurrence will then be infinitely good rather than infinitely bad.

The shepherd and the snake together can be seen as a degenerate form of the *ouroboros*, the ancient symbol of a serpent biting its own tail, representing cyclicality and rebirth. Nietzsche was familiar with this symbol, occasionally alluding to it, as Loeb (2010) notes. As the shepherd and snake's mouths are together and no circle is formed, this would be a monstrously failed ouroboros, more suited to representing something horrible. Zarathustra accordingly fails to accept the eternal recurrence with the snake in his mouth choking him. But at the end of the vision, he sees that overcoming his disgust would allow him to accept the eternal recurrence.

This vision of redemption lifts Zarathustra's spirits. At the beginning of the next section, he finally has "overcome all his pain," and can reflect on his own emotional journey concerning the eternal recurrence. He recalls how it was foreshadowed by "the wanderer's shadow and the longest boredom and the stillest hour – they all urged me: 'It is high time.'" As the wanderer's shadow says that it is high time in "On Great Events," these remarks confirm that the eternal recurrence is being foreshadowed as early as that section. Whilethe phrase "longest boredom" [*längste Weile*] doesn't appear anywhere else in the text, it might refer to the great weariness prophesied by the soothsayer in Part II. His stillest hour encouraged him to speak of the eternal recurrence. He recognizes his own struggle to even conceive of it, saying "Thus everything called out to me in signs: 'It is time!' But I did not hear, until at last my abyss stirred and my thought bit me." (Z III: "On Involuntary Bliss").

Though Zarathustra is not ready to face the eternal recurrence of everything bad that has ever happened, he can imagine doing so: "Alas, abysmal thought that is my thought, when shall I find the strength to hear you burrowing, without trembling anymore?" Though he admits that he still lacks this strength, he tells his abysmal thought, "Your gravity was always terrible enough for me; but one day I shall yet find the strength and the lion's voice to summon you. And once I have overcome myself that far, then I also want to overcome myself in what is still greater; and a victory shall seal my perfection" (Z III: "On Involuntary Bliss").

This section continues after "Thus spoke Zarathustra." As night falls, Zarathustra expects his horror at the eternal recurrence to overtake him. Happily, things are otherwise: "And he waited for his unhappiness the entire night, but he waited in vain. The night remained bright and still, and happiness itself came closer and closer to him." Here Zarathustra is finally making mental contact with the infinite positive value of good things repeated forever, rather than infinite negative value. His concluding remark that "happiness is a woman" prefigures his improving sentiments toward life, wisdom, and eternity, which are personified as women elsewhere in the book, as will soon be discussed (Z III: "On Involuntary Bliss").

In the next section, Zarathustra speaks to the sky before dawn: "O heaven above me, pure and deep! You abyss of light! Seeing you, I tremble with godlike desires. To throw myself into your height, that is *my* depth." Though mountain peaks and abysses were Zarathustra's previous metaphors for the heights and depths of value, he now considers the height of the heavens above, a metaphor for the infinities of value that he is slowly becoming able to contemplate. Near the end of the section, he describes his discovery of these infinities and his inability to speak clearly of them in suitably cryptic language: "The world is deep – and deeper than day had ever been aware. Not everything may be put into words in the presence of the day." Here as in the dream from "The Soothsayer," "day" corresponds to the period during which human life exists, between the cycles of recurrence. (Z III: "Before Sunrise").

This is the final section at sea. The next four sections present Zarathustra's commentary on human society as he wanders home. The following four sections express his private reflections in his mountaintop cave. After these eight sections, Zarathustra is finally able to confront his abysmal thought.

8 "The Convalescent" Has Animals Proclaiming Recurrence

One morning in his cave, Zarathustra finds the lion's voice to confront his abysmal thought. Like a lion, he roars so loudly that animals in nearby caves flee in terror. His own animals rush to his side, fearful for him. He calls out a lengthy challenge that ends with "I, Zarathustra, the advocate of life, the advocate of suffering, the advocate of the circle; I summon you, my most abysmal thought!" He greets this thought as it arrives: "Hail to me! You are coming, I hear you. My abyss speaks, I have turned my ultimate depth inside out into the light. Hail to me! Come here! Give me your hand! Huh! Let go! Huhhuh! Nausea, nausea, nausea – woe unto me!" (Z III: "The Convalescent" 1).

Nauseated by the thought of all that is bad recurring eternally, Zarathustra loses consciousness. For seven days after regaining his senses, he doesn't eat, drink, or speak, though his animals find food for him. Finally, he sits up and enjoys the scent of a rose-apple. The animals gather around and encourage him toward recovery, saying "Step outside your cave: the world awaits you like a garden" (Z III: "The Convalescent" 2).

Zarathustra tells them to "chatter on like this and let me listen . . . where there is chattering, the world lies before me like a garden." Here he isn't engaging with the substance of their thoughts, but falling back into his own experiences of the sounds they make. His broader point is about the separateness of minds from each other: "for every soul, every other soul is an afterworld. Precisely between what is most similar, illusion lies most beautifully; for the smallest cleft is the hardest to bridge" (Z III: "The Convalescent" 2).

While the separateness of minds might seem a surprising topic of discussion here, it may have helped Zarathustra confront his abysmal thought. One way to deal with contemptible people – and in Zarathustra's case, their eternal recurrence – is to get some emotional distance from them by focusing on yourself. This seems to be part of what Zarathustra has done, and he will spend the next section conversing with his own soul. Though he remains turned inward, the words of his animals please him much more than his thoughts of contemptible people did. He enjoys them as sounds rather than as representations of thoughts in other minds.

The animals then begin proclaiming the eternal recurrence, saying "Everything goes, everything comes back; eternally rolls the wheel of being. Everything dies, everything blossoms again; eternally runs the year of being." Zarathustra acknowledges their understanding of the eternal recurrence and his emotional drama surrounding it, saying "O you buffoons and barrel organs . . . How well you know what had to be fulfilled in seven days, and how that monster crawled down my throat and suffocated me. But I bit off its head and spewed it out." Struck by their nonchalance about it, he asks "And you, have you already made a hurdy-gurdy song of this?" The hurdy-gurdy was a *declasse* instrument often played by beggars. Zarathustra is taken aback at how easily the animals accept the idea for which he paid a great emotional price. He continues, "But now I lie here, still weary of this biting and spewing, still sick from my own redemption. *And you watched all this?*" (Z III: "The Convalescent" 2). He wonders if they watched his anguish in a spirit of cruelty. They of course did not – they feared for him when they heard him roar, and brought him food while he was unconscious.

Zarathustra concludes this soliloquy by expressing his abysmal thought: "All-too-small, the greatest – that was my disgust with man. And the eternal recurrence even of the smallest – that was my disgust with all existence. Alas! Nausea! Nausea! Nausea!" His animals again get it right: "Do not speak on, O convalescent . . . singing is for the convalescent; the healthy can speak. And when the healthy man also wants songs, he wants different songs from the convalescent." As the section title indicates, Zarathustra hasn't returned to full mental health. He again smiles, calls the animals "buffoons and barrel organs," and agrees with them: "How well you know what comfort I invented for myself in seven days! That I must sing again, this comfort and convalescence I invented for myself. Must you immediately turn this too into a hurdy-gurdy song [*Leier-Lied*]?" (Z III: "The Convalescent" 2).

The animals tell him to make a new lyre for himself and sing new songs to cure his soul, as he will soon do.[34] They call him "*the teacher of the eternal recurrence*" and proclaim "that all things recur eternally, and we ourselves too; and that we have already existed an eternal number of times, and all things with us." They then describe how he will proclaim the eternal recurrence when he dies:

> 'Now I die and vanish,' you would say, 'and all at once I am nothing. The soul is as mortal as the body. But the knot of causes in which I am entangled recurs and will create me again. I myself belong to the causes of the eternal recurrence. I come again, with this sun, with this earth, with this eagle, with this serpent – not to a new life or a better life or a similar life: I come back eternally to this same, selfsame life, in what is greatest as in what is smallest, to teach again the eternal recurrence of all things, to speak again the word of the great noon of earth and man, to proclaim the superhuman again to men. I spoke my word, I break of my word: thus my eternal lot wants it; as a proclaimer I perish. The hour has now come when he who goes under should bless himself. Thus *ends* Zarathustra's going under.' (Z III: "The Convalescent" 2).

Zarathustra doesn't reply, falling into a silent conversation with his soul. With Zarathustra silent, the eagle and serpent "honored the great stillness around him and cautiously stole away" (Z III: "The Convalescent" 2).

There is considerable debate about whether the animals present the eternal recurrence accurately. Kathleen Higgins (1987), Laurence Lampert (1986), Lawrence Hatab (2005), and Paul Loeb (2010) rightly trust the animals' presentation of the doctrine. Those who doubt the animals neglect the narrative context of Zarathustra's decisive battle with his abysmal thought.[35] In calling the animals "buffoons and barrel organs," he isn't chiding them for an erroneous account of eternal recurrence, but responding to their easy acceptance of a doctrine that he could accept only after an emotional struggle that left him comatose and then unable to stand or speak for seven days (Z III: "The Convalescent" 2). He is a convalescent recovering from this struggle with his abysmal thought, while his animals speak from the perspective of full emotional and mental health. References to convalescents throughout the book treat them as improving but having further progress to make, as the metaphor of convalescence directly indicates.

---

[34] Edwards (2015) suggests that *Leier* refers to the ancient lyre, a more respected instrument than the hurdy-gurdy. Burnham and Jesinghausen (2010) note that it is a symbol of Apollo rather than Dionysus.

[35] For example, Strong (1975), Deleuze (1983), Nehamas (1985), Heidegger (1991), Berkowitz (1995), McNeil (2020), and Fogarty (2022).

Zarathustra's remarks outside this section testify to the animals' general trustworthiness, especially his eagle and serpent. He concludes the Prologue by describing them as "The proudest animal under the sun and the wisest animal under the sun" (25), and wishing he had the serpent's wisdom. Apart from his continual references to them as "buffoons and barrel organs," the most critical remark he makes about them is at the beginning of Part IV, when he misleads them in order to go up to his mountaintop alone, saying "Up here I may speak more freely than before hermits' caves and hermits' domestic animals" (Z IV: "The Honey Sacrifice"). But this need not suggest doubting the animals. We aren't always able to speak freely about everything, even around intelligent people whom we love. And as we'll see, even in that section the animals are right in the end, as he actually does what he claims to have misled them about doing. Subsequent references to the animals are uniformly positive. Later when hearing someone praise cows, Zarathustra replies, "You should also see *my* animals, my eagle and my serpent: their like is not to be found on earth today" (Z IV: "The Voluntary Beggar"). Often during the subsequent dinner party, he favors the company of his animals over the higher men. In the final section, he hears the cry of his eagle above and says, "You are the right animals for me; I love you" (Z IV: "The Sign").

Nietzsche describes *Zarathustra* as a tragedy, and the animals are its chorus. Like a Greek chorus, they all speak with a single voice. Nietzsche's preview of the book's first subsection in *The Gay Science* under the title "*Incipit tragoedia*" introduces them, with Zarathustra speaking to the sun of "my eagle and my serpent" (GS 342). In the *Birth of Tragedy*, Nietzsche describes members of a chorus as "fictitious *creatures of nature*" (BT 7), a description that applies with impressive literality to the talking animals of *Zarathustra*.

As the animals describe the eternal recurrence as a "wheel" and a "ring," their doubters often reject their representation of it as a circle.[36] Gilles Deleuze (1983) for example writes, "On two occasions in *Zarathustra* Nietzsche explicitly denies that the eternal return is **a** circle which makes the same return" (xi). The other occasion seems to concern the dwarf's remark that "time itself is a circle" (Z II: "The Vision and the Riddle").[37] Deleuze neglects the narrative context of Zarathustra's emotional state in having to confront the infinite horror of bad things recurring eternally. The dwarf is the spirit of gravity, trying to bring Zarathustra down. He describes the eternal recurrence accurately in order to stir

---

[36] The animals are in circles when we first meet them in Z Prologue 10: "An eagle soared through the sky in wide circles, and on him there hung a serpent, not like prey but like a friend: For she kept herself wound around her neck." I thank Wen Ling Chia for this insight. See also Burnham and Jesinghausen (2010).

[37] See Mollison (2023) for discussion. Rayman (2022) similarly doubts a circular conception.

up Zarathustra's negative emotions. Zarathustra's angry reply isn't responding to the truth of the dwarf's claim, but instead to the hurtful intention with which it was made. When the animals describe the eternal recurrence at length, Zarathustra agrees but is taken aback at their nonchalance toward infinite negative value. It remains unclear how Deleuze would account for Zarathustra's own references to himself as "the advocate of the circle" (Z III: "The Convalescent" 1).

The animals' account rules out selective accounts of the eternal recurrence, such as Deleuze's view that "reactive forces will not return.[38] The small, petty, reactive man will not return" (71). As they explain, what is smallest will return along with what is greatest, and everything will come back exactly the same as it was. Deleuze cites KSA 11:26[376] where Nietzsche says that "other modes of thought will ultimately perish" from the eternal recurrence, but this seems to be a short-term effect of widespread belief in it, rather than any important structural feature of the eternal recurrence itself (WP 1053). Nietzsche notes that views assigning negative value to life, when combined with eternal recurrence, assign infinite negative value to our total existence. It would be hard for humans to go on believing that their condition is so hellish, so these views will decline. But the next cycle of recurrence will bring them back, only to decline again.

The linear presentation of eternal recurrence in "On the Vision and the Riddle," with what seems to be an infinite straight line, is consistent with the circular presentation elsewhere.[39] Lines and circles are largely equivalent for representing the temporal structure of the eternal recurrence. The same recurring events can be represented either as a circle or as an infinitely repeating line. To turn linear time into circular time, wind up the infinite timeline into a circle. To turn circular time into linear time, unwind the time-circle into a line of infinitely repeating segments. While a circle and an infinite line might differ as seen from the outside, they are the same as experienced from the inside, and we can observe life only from within life itself. From the inside, passing through an infinite series of identical snakes is indistinguishable from an infinite circular journey through an ouroboros. As Hatab (2005) writes, "'deciding' between a linear and a cyclical course of time" is *unnecessary* in coming to terms with Nietzsche's thinking on this matter" (72).

As Joshua Rayman (2022) notes, ellipses and "other shapes that return on themselves" (58) can suggest the same temporal structure as a circle. Perhaps Nietzsche doesn't invoke these other shapes because their additional geometric structure doesn't correspond to anything he wants to convey. Ellipses and

---

[38] Including Dombowsky (1997).

[39] Loeb (2010) notes that this apparent line might itself be a very large circle.

squares return on themselves, but what would elongation or four corners signify? Circles and infinite lines, described by the simplest equations in polar and Cartesian coordinates respectively, provide less complicated metaphors for recurrence.

Circles might better depict the sort of identity needed for us to eternally return as the same individuals than lines. As one goes around and around the circle, one's lives begin at the same point. As one goes along the infinite line, one's lives begin at different points. Infinite lines are however consistent with recurrence, as the same thing can eternally recur along the infinite line. Dan Korman (2015) discusses the example of a low-lying island when tides or longer-term sea levels rise and fall. An island may cease to exist as the waters rise and later exist again as the waters fall. If we are like islands, the dots of our existence on an infinite line might represent our eternal recurrence. Whether Nietzsche accepted this point or saw infinite lines as suitable representations of recurrence is unclear. It would be overly optimistic to treat his discussion of blessed isles or mountains coming out of the sea as recognition of how islands can go in and out of existence. Circles less ambiguously represent recurrence.

Georg Simmel (1920) argues that my current self and the identical person in the next cycle aren't the same person.[40] He thinks this could be true only "if the same ego were present in both. But in reality I do not return, but a phenomenon appears which is identical with me in all of its traits and experiences" (174). Paul Loeb (2022) replies that Nietzsche has in mind qualitative identity rather than numerical identity – being perfect duplicates, rather than being one and the same person. While qualitative identity is indeed what the eternal recurrence most straightforwardly supports, it may even support numerical identity, if we return to existence like islands in rising and falling seas.

Simmel would object that such recurrence doesn't bring back a numerically identical ego. But Nietzsche rejects Simmel's premise that we have personal identity by having an ego that is irreducible to our other physical parts (BGE Pref 16). Derek Parfit's (1984) psychological reductionism seems much more like Nietzsche's view.[41] Parfit holds that if I step into a *Star Trek* teletransporter that disintegrates me and sends all the information about my physical structure elsewhere so that an exact duplicate of myself is recreated there, that's as good as ordinary survival, as my psychological states are preserved. An irreducible ego might not survive teletransportation. But that's fine according to Parfit, since I never had an irreducible ego anyway. As Nietzsche too rejects the irreducible ego, he can treat the eternal recurrence much like Parfit treats teletransportation.

---

[40] See also Magnus (1978).

[41] As Remhof (2021) suggests, Nietzsche has views on such metaphysical questions.

What persists of oneself in dying and existing again might be called one's soul. The animals' proclamation of the eternal recurrence accordingly leads Zarathustra to converse happily with his soul throughout the following section, "The Great Longing." While souls are often conceived along the lines of the irreducible ego, Zarathustra favors a more reductionist view. Earlier he says, "body am I entirely, and nothing else; and soul is only a word for something about the body"[42] (Z I: "Despisers of the Body"). Such reductionism might identify the soul with psychological states which are reducible to bodily states. Then the persistence of the soul across time might be the counterfactual dependence of psychological states at later times on those at earlier times.

Determinism favors continuity of personal identity across different cycles of recurrence, by allowing the right sort of dependence between them. The animals indicate Nietzsche's deterministic assumptions with their reference to a "knot of causes" (Z III: "The Convalescent"). In Nietzsche's deterministic recurrence (though not in Poincaré's indeterministic recurrence), facts about future selves counterfactually depend on facts about past selves. A different past life would've deterministically generated different future lives, and this present life might not have come to pass. This resembles the dependences between past and future psychological states within a single life – between my high-school-era fascination with *Zarathustra*, my undergraduate enthusiasm for Nietzsche, my PhD-era appetite for projects like *Nietzsche and Morality*, and my current motivation to write this Element. Many different things can explain this dependence – the natural persistence of one's desires across time, past states of the universe determining far future states, or a *Star Trek* teletransporter. If counterfactual dependence across time is a key ingredient for identity, all these things provide it.

Simmel's final objection is that identity doesn't hold between spatially separate duplicates, and therefore won't hold between temporally separate duplicates:

> If many absolutely identical worlds exist in space, but there is no communication among them, then the content of my ego would be repeated identically in each of them. Yet I would not be entitled to say that I live in each of these worlds. And it is obvious that these identical persons living alongside one another would behave in the same way as persons living successively, as they do according to the doctrine of eternal recurrence. (174)

Simmel is right that these spatially separated duplicates aren't the same person. But this is no obstacle to treating temporally separated duplicates as the same person. Spatial and temporal separation have different consequences for

---

[42] See Sinhababu (2022).

identity. Let's return to the example of an island amidst rising and falling seas. A second duplicate world will contain a second duplicate island that isn't numerically identical to the first. Islands in different worlds can't be one and the same island. But as the seas of each world rise and fall, the island in that world can cease to exist and then return to existence as the same island. Islands at different times, even with a gap in between where no island exists, can be one and the same island.

Simmel's arguments fail to show that cycles of recurrence disrupt personal identity. We might still return from nonexistence to existence as islands do. Parfit's arguments moreover favor Nietzsche's view of personal identity over Simmel's. When the animals envision Zarathustra saying, "I come again, with this sun, with this earth, with this eagle, with this serpent – not to a new life or a better life or a similar life: I come back eternally to this same, selfsame life," the eternal recurrence might indeed make his statement true (Z III: "The Convalescent").

9 "The Other Dancing Song" Expresses Love of Life

At the end of Zarathustra's conversation with his soul, he encourages his soul to sing. His soul accordingly sings a song to which he dances with Life, personified as a woman. (Here capitalization will distinguish Life personified as a woman from life the period between birth and death. Zarathustra's other loves, Wisdom and Eternity, are capitalized similarly.)

Zarathustra has encountered Life before in "The Dancing Song," which stands in the middle of a three-section sequence of songs that end "Thus sang Zarathustra." These songs, which appear in Part II several sections before "The Soothsayer," provide useful context for "The Other Dancing Song" and the overall story of Zarathustra's engagement with the eternal recurrence. So it will be helpful to consider them first.

The first of these three earlier sections is "The Night Song." Here Zarathustra describes himself metaphorically as light rather than nocturnal darkness, and as a giver rather than a receiver. He sings of how he wishes to be like the darkness and receive. The metaphorical connection between light and giving is familiar from the beginning of the *Prologue*, where Zarathustra wishes to be like the sun and give his light to the world below. What he actually gives the world below is his philosophy, beginning with his message of the superhuman. If giving and being like the light symbolizes teaching philosophy, his wish here to receive and be like the night would indicate a desire to learn more philosophy. What he has learned of the eternal recurrence since then might then count as satisfying his wish. This section furthermore includes the sentence "There is a cleft between giving and receiving; and the narrowest cleft is the last to be bridged" (Z II: "The Night Song"). This discussion of narrow clefts is repeated in "The Convalescent," in reference to his conversation with the animals. In both sections, it indicates how separate minds can be despite communicating with each other.

"The Dancing Song" begins with Zarathustra meeting girls who are dancing in a forest. He sings a song for them to dance to, announcing that his song will mock the spirit of gravity, his "supreme and most powerful devil." He has mentioned this enemy once long before – "And when I saw my devil I found him serious, thorough, profound, and solemn: it was the spirit of gravity – through him all things fall" (Z I: "On Reading and Writing"). While the song doesn't mention the spirit of gravity by name, the earlier section suggests that the girls' dancing itself opposes the spirit of gravity: "I would believe only in a god who could dance. And when I saw my devil I found him serious, thorough, profound, and solemn: it was the spirit of gravity – through him all things fall. Not by wrath does one kill but by laughter. Come, let us kill the spirit of gravity!" (Z II: "The Dancing Song").

Zarathustra's song is about Life and Wisdom, personified as his romantic partners. Within that metaphor, he describes himself as a fish whom Life has caught with her "golden fishing rod." Life rejects his flattering description of herself as "unfathomable," saying "Thus runs the speech of all fish . . . what *they* do not fathom is unfathomable." She furthermore describes herself as "merely changeable and wild and a woman in every way, and not virtuous – even if you men call me profound, faithful, eternal, and mysterious. But you men always present us with your own virtues, O you virtuous men!" (Z II: "The Dancing Song"). The message Life expresses in her self-deprecating rejection of Zarathustra's flattery is that our lives have their good and bad parts, and that Zarathustra's life-affirming philosophy is largely a reflection of his own long-standing and intense love of life. Because of this love, he continues praising life even in hard times.

Indeed, this is how Wisdom angrily explains away Zarathustra's love of life: "You will, you want, you love – that is the only reason why you praise life." Zarathustra doesn't disagree and admits that he loves life alone. He comes close to telling wisdom this, but does not, as "there is no more wicked answer than telling one's wisdom the truth." As he explains, "thus matters stand among the three of us: Deeply I love only life – and verily, most of all when I hate life" (Z II: "The Dancing Song").

An intriguing feature of Zarathustra's complicated romantic relationship is that his love of Wisdom results from her similarity to Life. He says, "that I am well disposed toward wisdom, and often too well, that is because she reminds me so much of life. She has her eyes, her laugh, and even her little golden fishing rod: is it my fault that the two look so similar?" Life herself has confirmed this similarity, after asking Zarathustra, "Who is this wisdom?" Zarathustra "answered fervently,"

> Oh yes, wisdom! One thirsts after her and is never satisfied; one looks through veils, one grabs through nets. Is she beautiful? How should I know? But even the oldest carps are baited with her. She is changeable and stubborn; often I have seen her bite her lip and comb her hair against the grain. Perhaps she is evil and false and a female in every way; but just when she speaks ill of herself she is most seductive (Z II: "The Dancing Song").

Upon hearing this, Life "laughed sarcastically and closed her eyes." She then asked rhetorically, "Of whom are you speaking?", and answered "no doubt, of me" (Z II: "The Dancing Song").

The similarity between Life and Wisdom is explained by Zarathustra's life as a philosopher – etymologically, a lover of wisdom. The ups and downs of loving wisdom are therefore the ups and downs of his life. Life is therefore right to identify herself with Wisdom. And as Zarathustra enthusiastically advocates a life-affirming philosophy, it is indeed true that his love of Wisdom results from her similarity to Life.

Zarathustra's fervent answer to Life's question about Wisdom describes philosophers' pursuit of truth. Within the metaphor of men as fish, "the oldest carps" for which Wisdom is bait are ancient philosophers (Z II: "The Dancing Song"). The unsatisfied thirst and the veils and nets allude to epistemological difficulties in attaining the truths that philosophers seek. The same epistemological difficulties prevent Zarathustra from knowing whether Wisdom is beautiful. For Wisdom to speak ill of herself is for philosophy itself to cast doubt on the possibility or value of attaining truth. This is a topic of considerable interest to Nietzsche, discussed for example in the first book of *Beyond Good and Evil*. His interest in writing about it is a sense in which he finds Wisdom's speaking ill of herself especially attractive.

Eventually, after the sun has long set, the girls go home and the merry singing and dancing ends. Amidst the darkness, Zarathustra grows sad. Even after his love song to Life, questions about the purpose of life come to him, from a mysterious source. "Something unknown is around me and looks thoughtful. What? Are you still alive, Zarathustra? Why? What for? By what? Whither? Where? How? Is it not folly still to be alive?" In the dream he will soon have of being death's night watchman, dark hours represent periods when nothing is alive. This makes the darkness after his dance with life a natural time for recognizing the impermanence of everything mortals can achieve, and for questioning how life could even come into being. He furthermore attributes these questions to night itself – "the evening that asks thus through me" – asking his friends to forgive his sadness (Z II: "The Dancing Song"). This seems to be an early premonition of the eternal recurrence. While it's too subtle to make Zarathustra think of the cosmology of recurrence, it suggests the same negative attitude toward life that the soothsayer's prophecy does.

Zarathustra's questions and his accompanying sadness lead into the next section, set on an adjacent isle of tombs. Here Zarathustra laments the sorrows of his past. Describing beautiful things he loved, he tells how they were destroyed by enemies who "murdered the visions and dearest wonders of my youth." Nietzsche's own enthusiasm and subsequent disappointment regarding the composer Richard Wagner seems to be among these lamentations: "And once I wanted to dance as I had never danced before: over all the heavens I wanted to dance. Then you persuaded my dearest singer. And he struck up a horrible dismal tune" (Z II: "The Tomb Song"). Read in the context of the previous section, Zarathustra's enemies seem to be abstractions like the spirit of gravity, which exercise their influence over the culture of his era. The reference to tombs full of dead things from the past looks forward to the tombs he guarded as night watchman in "The Soothsayer," and foreshadows the dark significance of willing the eternal recurrence. To do so would be to will the creation and murder of all these things he loved, an infinite number of times.

With this background from previous songs, and especially the details of Zarathustra's relationship with Life and Wisdom, "The Other Dancing Song" can be better understood. The song begins with Zarathustra's delight as he looks into Life's eyes. But Life is of course not always so delightful, as she honestly told Zarathustra before. The song to which they dance accordingly describes how happiness and suffering are intertwined: "I fear you near, I love you far; your flight lures me; your seeking cures me: I suffer, but what would I not gladly suffer for you?" Their dance is violent, with Life slapping him at one point – "In my face two red blotches from your hand itch" (Z III: "The Other Dancing Song" 1). Zarathustra responds by angrily cracking his whip.

Life finally calls this fierce dance to an end, asking Zarathustra not to crack his whip anymore, and pleading with him to end their conflict. She tells him, "Beyond good and evil we found our island and our green meadow – we two alone. Therefore we had better like each other."[43] While moral requirements might suggest going on with life even if one has no love for it, such require-ments have no force for two "good-for-nothings and evil-for-nothings," as Life

---

[43] I thank Kuong Un Teng for helpful discussion of this that contributed to Sinhababu and Teng (2019).

describes herself and Zarathustra (Z III: "The Other Dancing Song" 2). The value in a world without objective good and evil moreover takes the subjective form created by Zarathustra's love for life, and perhaps the form of the well-being that life gives him.

As Life then confides, Zarathustra's relationship with Wisdom explains part of her love for him: "And that I like you, often too well, that you know; and the reason is that I am jealous of your wisdom. Oh, this mad old fool of a wisdom! If your wisdom ever ran away from you, then my love would quickly run away from you too" (Z III: "The Other Dancing Song" 2). While the precise meta-phorical significance of these emotional complications is difficult to discern, it's clear that Zarathustra's pursuit of philosophy explains much of why Life is good to him. His life-affirming philosophical conclusions make life better for him, and his pursuit of wisdom provides his life with much of its meaning.

Life then says, "O Zarathustra, you are not faithful enough to me. You do not love me nearly as much as you say; I know you are thinking of leaving me soon." Zarathustra indeed is a mortal man, and must leave her. She tells him that they will soon hear a "heavy growl-bell" that sounds the hours between one o'clock and midnight, and again says "you want to leave me soon." Zarathustra says "Yes . . . but you also know –" and whispers something into her ear that the text does not disclose (Z III: "The Other Dancing Song" 2).

What Zarathustra whispers is heavily debated among interpreters. Michael Platt (1988) claims that he whispers that he will return, which I too accept.[44] As Gabriel Zamosc (2015) emphasizes, subsequent clues help us discern what Zarathustra whispers. Life replies "You know that, O Zarathustra? Nobody knows that." As they weep together looking over a green meadow, Zarathustra reflects "But then life was dearer to me than all my wisdom ever was" (Z III: "The Other Dancing Song" 2).

Nietzsche wishes for the eternal recurrence and recognizes that the evidence for it is insufficient. This is why Zarathustra only privately whispers that he will return. Life is right that nobody knows that they will return, eternally or even once. While infinite time favors eternal recurrence, Nietzsche was in no position to verify the other assumptions it requires. This is how the empirical evidence stands in our time, Nietzsche's time, and presumably Zarathustra's time. So no one's belief in the eternal recurrence has the level of justification required for knowledge, as Life herself asserts.

Nietzsche's recognition that he had insufficient evidence for the eternal recur-rence explains why he never endorses it in his own voice in the published works.

---

[44] Zamosc (2015) has him saying that Life is pregnant with his child, which might amount to the same thing. Lampert (1986) has Zarathustra adding that he will return eternally. These interpret-ations express ideas consistent with the evidence here, and go further.

Instead, fictional characters express it. The *Gay Science* has a hypothetical demon revealing it. *Zarathustra* largely presents it in dreams, visions, and speeches by talking animals, and is itself a work of fiction. Zarathustra is the character who expresses Nietzsche's views, and the text focuses more on his emotional reactions to the eternal recurrence than on the cosmology itself.

Whenever Zarathustra explicitly affirms that there will be an eternal recurrence, his voice falls to a whisper. At the gateway with the dwarf, Zarathustra spoke more and more softly as he went through the cosmological reasoning favoring eternal recurrence, "whispering of eternal things" until he reached the conclusion "must we not eternally return?" (Z II: "Vision and Riddle"). As the question mark indicates, his engagement with the cosmological hypothesis takes the noncommittal linguistic form of questions about whether it follows from premises including infinite time. When the scene shifts, the whispering itself is included among the key symbols of that section: "Where was the dwarf gone now? And the gateway? And the spider? And all the whispering?" (Z II: "Vision and Riddle"). The lack of volume with which he expresses belief in the eternal recurrence in both of these sections expresses Nietzsche's own lack of certainty about it. In "The Other Dancing Song," he claims to know of it, the most confident assertion of its reality that he ever makes in his own voice. The assertion is made in a whisper heard only by Life and never disclosed to us.

Zarathustra accepts the eternal recurrence only in noncommittal or unheard whispers because of Nietzsche's own uncertainty about it. His level of credence in the eternal recurrence was intermediate between belief and disbelief. While the nature of infinite time suggests the eternal recurrence, further assumptions that Nietzsche couldn't prove are also required. As a good naturalist, Nietzsche won't advocate an empirical hypothesis for which he knows the evidence is insufficient, or even have Zarathustra do so loudly. What Nietzsche is uncertain of, Zarathustra merely whispers. Here he expresses his belief in the eternal recurrence more confidently than he or Nietzsche do anywhere else in the published works, below our hearing.

What compels Zarathustra to say something that Nietzsche couldn't fully believe? As Zarathustra admits in his final reflection, his love of Life has overcome his love of Wisdom. He wants to be with Life, and wishful thinking has made him overconfident that the eternal recurrence will bring them together for eternity. "The Dancing Song" portrays his love of Wisdom as his will to philosophical truth, so Zarathustra is admitting that his intense love of Life has driven him to a philosophical view that his evidence doesn't fully support. Recognizing this deep uncertainty about whether their relationship will soon end forever or whether it will eternally recur, Zarathustra and Life weep together.

The best evidence for Nietzsche's uncertainty about the eternal recurrence is that he never offers an argument for it in his own voice in the published works. He left further clues of his uncertainty in *Zarathustra*. These include Zarathustra's mere whispers of the idea, Life's reply that he doesn't know it will happen, and Zarathustra's final reflection that Life is dearer to him than Wisdom. Nietzsche may have hoped that readers deciphering these clues would come to understand his uncertainty and longing for the eternal recurrence. If the interpretation here is correct, his hopes are now realized.

10 "Once More" and "The Drunken Song" Sing of Infinities

"The Other Dancing Song" concludes with a song about the eternal recurrence, accompanied by the strokes of a bell. Zarathustra calls it "Once More" [*Noch ein Mal*] when singing it later with his dinner guests. It is also called "Zarathustra's Round" [*Zarathustra's Rudgesang*], an apt name because of the cyclical structure of the eternal recurrence (Z IV: "The Drunken Song"). "Once More" has sometimes been set to music as the "Midnight-Song" [*Mitternachts-Lied*], an apt name because it begins by asking someone who has woken from sleep what deep midnight declares. The answer, expressed with depth as a metaphor for infinities and other vast quantities, is that the eternal recurrence makes infinities out of everything existing finitely within a single cycle. The song concludes by adopting the perspective of those moved to pursue infinite joy rather than to avoid infinite woe.

In "The Other Dancing Song," "Once More" consists in eleven phrases arranged between the words from "one" to "twelve," representing twelve strokes of a bell. These number words are best read like musical notes, representing twelve bellstrokes that mark midnight rather than actual words said by Zarathustra or anyone else. In the "The Drunken Song," Zarathustra offers a commentary on most of the lyrics. Then he and his guests sing all eleven lines together. These lyrics begin,

> O man, take care!
> What does the deep midnight declare?
> "I was asleep –
> From a deep dream I woke and swear: (Z III: "The Other Dancing Song" 3)

Word choice suggests that the deep dream [*tiefen Traum*] is Zarathustra's dream of being death's night watchman. This dream happens when he falls into a "deep sleep" [*tiefen Schlaf*], the only use of this phrase in the book (Z II: "The Soothsayer"). *Traum* is also applied to that dream, but not to other presentations of eternal recurrence such as the vision with the dwarf at the gateway.

In recounting that dream, Zarathustra says "the brightness of midnight was all around me" (Z II: "The Soothsayer"). Midnight [*Mitternacht*] in that dream represents the vast period in the cycle of recurrence when no life exists. If "midnight" refers collectively to all such periods, it is infinitely long. In any case, it deserves the epithet "deep midnight," with "deep" signifying its vastness whether finite and very long, or infinite.

"Deep" represents infinities and possibly other vast quantities. While depths are opposed to peaks and heights elsewhere in the text, this song invokes no distinctively upward elevations or contrasts them with depths. Especially as deep midnight is a large amount of time, "deep" must here encompass positive magnitudes. "Deep midnight" then can be defined as "the vast periods in the cycle of recurrence when life doesn't exist." Zarathustra's "deep dream" not only occurs in a deep sleep, but is about infinite things.

How then is deep midnight to declare anything, if there are no living beings in it to speak? A simple way is for events during deep midnight to have causal consequences. What deep midnight declares then is whatever the events of deep midnight cause. When we discover our eternally recurring existence among these causal consequences, we hear what deep midnight declares.

Zarathustra's commentary to his dinner guests reminds them where they stand in this causal history. First he says, "Do you not hear how it speaks secretly, terribly, cordially to you – the old deep, deep midnight?" (Z IV: "The Drunken Song" 3). Then he says, "This speech is for delicate ears, for your ears: *What does the deep midnight declare?*" (Z IV: "The Drunken Song" 4). The third and fourth lines which concern his sleep and the deep dream from "The Soothsayer" aren't repeated in the course of his commentary, though they do appear in the lyrics at the end. Perhaps in describing the eternal recurrence to his guests, there is no need to talk about the dream. Accordingly, his clearest references in the later discussion are to symbols from "On the Vision and the Riddle" – the dog, the moon, and the spider. That was the vision in which he most clearly saw what deep midnight declares, and whispered it for the first time himself.

The fifth and sixth lines articulate what deep midnight declares:

> The world is deep,
> Deeper than day had been aware (Z III: "The Other Dancing Song" 3).

As these causal consequences of one instance of midnight include everything in all the cycles of recurrence that come after, deep midnight indeed declares that the world is deep. Whatever exists in finite amounts during one cycle must exists in infinite amounts when summed across all cycles. As reality includes infinities of all these things, the world becomes deep, with the finite magnitudes of all things becoming infinite when summed over the infinite cycles of eternity.

If deep midnight consists in the vast lifeless periods during cycles of recurrence, day represents the periods during which living things exist. As Zarathustra is the discoverer of the eternal recurrence, no one in his cycle had previously recognized that the world was so deep as to include infinite magnitudes of everything. Those of his day had in this sense been unaware of the depth of the world. Zarathustra's later commentary on the depth of day describes infinite past happiness in olfactory terms: "A smell is secretly welling up, a fragrance and smell of eternity, a rose-blessed, brown gold-wine fragrance of old happiness" (Z IV: "The Drunken Song" 6).

The seventh and eighth lines consider emotional states that drive our attitudes toward the eternal recurrence:

> Deep is its woe;
> Joy – deeper yet than agony: (Z III: "The Other Dancing Song" 3).

The eternal recurrence gives all the woe and joy in a single cycle infinite depth. The eighth line can be sung by those who regard their lives as more full of joy than woe. When such lives eternally recur, the resulting eternal existence is infinitely more joyous than woeful. Zarathustra later explicates the seventh line from a perspective of wishing the day to end, saying "Leave me, you stupid, boorish, dumb day! Is not the midnight brighter?" It concludes by noting that however great the happiness and unhappiness of an eventful life might be, it falls far short of the infinities generated by the eternal recurrence: "reach for deeper happiness, for deeper unhappiness, reach for any god, do not reach for me: my unhappiness, my happiness is deep, you strange day, but I am yet no god, no god's hell: *deep is its woe*" (Z IV: "The Drunken Song" 7).

Zarathustra's later comments on the eighth line call deep midnight a "drunken poetess." She may be remembering all the past events that she will declare to recur eternally. Zarathustra says, "Her woe she ruminates in a dream, the old deep midnight, and even more her joy. For joy, even if woe is deep, *joy is deeper yet than agony*." (Z IV: "The Drunken Song" 8).

The ninth line describes how woe [*Weh*] drives one to wish for an end to existence, so one can depart from the misery of this world:

> Woe implores: Go! (Z III: "The Other Dancing Song" 3).

The woeful folk of the soothsayer's prophecy wish to escape from life, but will be pulled back into it forever by the eternal recurrence. Zarathustra later ascribes a more complex attitude toward all that suffers [*was leidet*], describing how it lives on for some purpose other than its own existence: "'I want heirs' – thus speaks all that suffers; 'I want children, I do not want *myself*'" (Z IV: "The Drunken Song" 9). Whatever differences there may be between the form of woe that tells us to go and the suffering that wishes to be compensated by creating something better, they both make one wish for something other than the continuation of one's current state.

The tenth and eleventh lines conclude by describing how joy makes one wish for the eternal recurrence of all things:

> But all joy wants eternity –
> Wants deep, wants deep eternity!" (Z III: "The Other Dancing Song" 3).

Zarathustra later emphasizes how joy can make one wish for the eternal recurrence of everything, including all of one's woe. From the premises that all joy "wants *itself*," and that this desire achieves greatest satisfaction if the eternal recurrence brings joy back infinite times, Zarathustra concludes that "the ring's will strives in it" (Z IV: "The Drunken Song" 11).

Zarathustra embraces the eternal recurrence in this spirit. Wanting more of a single joy is desiring it to recur, which makes everything causing its recurrence instrumentally desirable. Then the eternal recurrence of everything, including all woe, has some instrumental desirability. While this instrumental desire might be far weaker than one's aversions to all woe, all joy together might outweigh all woe, making eternal recurrence instrumentally desirable overall. And even a single small joy adds to the instrumental desirability of all things.

11 "The Seven Seals" Proposes Marriage to Eternity

The Element reaches its climax with Zarathustra singing of seven joys that make him love life, and wish for the eternal recurrence. First, as a soothsayer, he releases "lightning bolts that say Yes and laugh Yes" (Z III: "The Seven Seals" 1). Second, as an atheist and foe of Christianity, he loves to "blow moldy words to the wind" and "sit on broken churches" (Z III: "The Seven Seals" 2). Third, as a creator, he has "laughed the laughter of creative lightning which is followed obediently but grumblingly by the long thunder of the deed" (Z III: "The Seven Seals" 3). Fourth, appreciating the evaluative complexity of the world, he drinks "full drafts from that foaming spice-and blend-mug in which all things are well blended" (Z III: "The Seven Seals" 4). Fifth, as a seafarer, he experiences "delight in searching which drives the sails toward the undiscovered" (Z III: "The Seven Seals" 5). Sixth, as a dancer he has often "jumped with both feet into golden-emerald delight" (Z III: "The Seven Seals" 6). Seventh and finally, he has soared like a bird "on my own wings into my own skies" (Z III: "The Seven Seals" 7).

These joys of life make Zarathustra wish for the eternal recurrence, here metaphorically represented as marriage to Eternity. After each of these seven affirmations he rhetorically asks, "Oh, how should I not lust after eternity and after the nuptial ring of rings, the ring of recurrence?" He concludes all seven by calling Eternity the only woman with whom he has ever wanted children, and announcing *"For I love you, O eternity!"* (Z III: "The Seven Seals").

While Zarathustra uses "Eternity" as a proper name for a woman for the first time in "The Seven Seals," the woman he speaks of has already appeared under her maiden name, "Life." Marriage makes romantic relationships officially permanent, and Zarathustra desires the eternal recurrence because it will make his relationship with Life permanent. He wants more than a brief fling with Life – he wants to be with her forever.

Zarathustra's profession of overwhelming love for Life in "The Other Dancing Song" is separated from "The Seven Seals" only by the brief musical interlude of "Once More" which Life herself mentions, so these passages are naturally read together. The love expressed in the former section drives him to propose marriage in the latter section. He wishes to wear the nuptial ring of recurrence, and become Life's husband. This means that he and Life will rejoin each other again and again over the course of infinite time. The married name "Eternity" will therefore befit her. The children arising from a universal Zarathustra's marriage to Eternity might be all the individual Zarathustras, and perhaps all the future Lifes.

"The Dancing Song" identifies Life with Wisdom. "The Seven Seals" identifies Life with Eternity. All three women whom Zarathustra loves are therefore one. This is not the first time that three persons of great cosmic significance have been presented as one. Traditional Christian doctrine, and especially Catholicism, emphasize the unity of the Father, the Son, and the Holy Spirit. To the Trinity of Christianity, Zarathustra opposes Wisdom, Life, and Eternity.

The trinities can be matched one-to-one. The vastness of Eternity corresponds to the transcendent nature of the Father, which makes sense if Eternity and a universal Zarathustra beget all the individual Zarathustras and Lifes. Life corresponds to the Son, who lived a mortal life. Wisdom might be the Holy Spirit, who proceeds in the world, as Zarathustra's philosophy does. Laurence Lampert (1986) and others note correspondences between "The Seven Seals" and Christian doctrine, among which a new Trinity would fit well.

As Lampert describes, the section title recalls the prophecy from the Biblical book of *Revelation*, in which the breaking of seven seals unleashes the apocalypse. When the first four seals are broken, the four horsemen of the apocalypse appear. Breaking the seventh seal readies angels to pour God's wrath upon the world, leading to its destruction. Numerological connections to *Revelation* run deep in *Zarathustra*. *Part I* and *Part II* of *Zarathustra* have twenty-two sections, just like *Revelation*, and if the seven seals of this sixteenth section are promoted to the status of sections themselves, *Part III* will have twenty-two sections as well. The three parts of *Zarathustra* will then have sixty-six sections, corresponding to the sixty-six books of the Bible.

Observing the structural similarities with *Revelation* leads Lampert to read a message of destruction into "The Seven Seals." He writes that Zarathustra "brings not peace but a sword" and is a "bringer of destruction" (241), perhaps like the horsemen and angels of the apocalypse. But the textual evidence offered for this reading largely comes from outside *Zarathustra*, rather than from this section. He acknowledges that "Grim vengeance does not intrude into what is shown of the seven seals" (241).

As Gudrun von Tevenar (2013) describes, Zarathustra's expression of love is in fact a reversal of the message of destruction in *Revelation*. She calls this section "a jubilant celebration of conquest, joy, lust, and desire." While *Revelation*'s apocalyptic prophecy describes the destruction of our earthly reality and its replacement by a new reality that God creates, Zarathustra wishes for our reality to recur and be regenerated eternally. The alternative title of "The Yes and Amen Song" expresses Zarathustra's accepting attitude toward the world. He says Yes to an eternal relationship with Life as he has known her. Rather than wishing for the destruction of the reality he has known, he says "so be it," the literal meaning of "amen" (Z III: "The Seven Seals").

Von Tevenar describes Zarathustra's love song as peculiar in two ways.[45] First, "it lacks customary tenderness" (290). While this is in some respects true, Zarathustra does tell Life (and therefore Eternity) how lovely she is in seven different ways. Perhaps describing the things that make one love one's life constitutes affectionate language when speaking to Life herself.

Second, when Zarathustra expresses his "lust for eternity," the word translated as 'lust' is

> '*brünstig*', which in this context is somewhat offensive. *Brünstig* is not a word usually used for human sexuality – it refers only to animals. Male animals during the rutting season are said to be *brünstig* and only for females which are 'on heat', that is, ready to conceive. As such, *brünstig* has little to do with either sexual desire or love; it is simply the entirely instinctive animal imperative to mate, and to mate only 'in season' when conception is possible. (290)

Perhaps it properly conveys the somewhat offensive and bestial character of *brünstig* to describe Zarathustra as horny for Eternity. As von Tevenar notes, Nietzsche describes himself as writing *Zarathustra* to express a counter-ideal to

---

[45] Shepherd (2018) and Zamosc (2022) also discuss Zarathustra's love for eternity.

the ascetic ideal (GM II: 25, EH: 'Genealogy of Morals'). Zarathustra's *brünstig* for Eternity certainly is counter to any ascetic ideal. It's still consistent with conventional romantic ideals, as it makes him eager to marry Eternity and father her children.

In characterizing *Zarathustra*, von Tevenar also notes that Nietzsche describes it as a parody in GS Pref 1. And what a parody of the Trinity! Seeking eternal bliss in the afterlife, Christians worship a God who is the Father, the Son, and the Holy Spirit. Wanting his earthly life to recur eternally, Zarathustra lusts for a woman who is Life, Wisdom, and Eternity.

12 Part IV Pits Zarathustra against the Soothsayer

The first section of Part IV begins after "months and years passed over Zarathustra's soul" and "his hair turned white." He has remained contentedly in the mountains for those months and years, and his animals describe him as lying in a "sky-blue lake of happiness." He explains his happiness in terms of "the *honey* in my veins that makes my blood thicker and my soul calmer," and tells his animals that he will go to the mountaintop to offer the honey sacrifice. After sending his animals back, he calls his talk of a honey sacrifice "mere cunning, and verily a useful folly" so that he could be alone and speak freely. He then describes his plans to catch men with a "fishing rod," the same metaphor applied to Life and Wisdom attracting their devotees before (Z IV: "The Honey Sacrifice"). Part IV is largely about how he meets these men and invites them back to his cave for a dinner party, which ends with their singing out a wish for the recurrence of all their lives.

Paul Loeb (2010, 2015) argues that the events of Part IV actually take place within Part III. He more specifically locates Part IV within "On Old and New Tablets," immediately before subsection 6 where Zarathustra addresses his "brothers," and a section before Zarathustra confronts his abysmal thought. While Loeb's interpretation has the appealing consequence that the story ends with the expression of love for Eternity in "The Seven Seals," Matthew Meyer (forthcoming) is right that the text speaks against it overall. There is no clear indication that years suddenly pass at that point in Part III, or that Zarathustra's hair changes color.

Most importantly, placing Part IV before Zarathustra's climactic struggle with his abysmal thought in "The Convalescent" throws his emotional development toward the eternal recurrence into disorder. In Part IV, he teaches the higher men of the eternal recurrence in "The Drunken Song" and leads them in singing "Once More" without any emotional upheaval of his own. We would expect more ambivalence about this idea if he hadn't yet overcome his abysmal thought. He wouldn't be able to sing of eternity before this overcoming, and he wouldn't need to fight a seven-day battle with his abysmal thought after singing so joyously of it.

Near the end of this section, Zarathustra announces an intention to sacrifice some of the best honey of his heart as bait for the men he wishes to catch. He says, "Out, out, my fishing rod! Down, down, bait of my happiness! Drip your sweetest dew, honey of my heart! Bite, my fishing rod, into the belly of all black melancholy!" Even if he spoke of a "honey sacrifice" to mislead the animals, they end up being right (Z IV: "The Honey Sacrifice"). This further confirms that the animals should be trusted even when Zarathustra makes seemingly critical remarks about them. The first sentence of the next section accordingly notes that "Zarathustra had spent and squandered the old honey down to the last drop" (Z IV: "The Cry of Distress").

The soothsayer from Part II then makes a surprising and disquieting experience at Zarathustra's mountaintop cave. He is described here as "the proclaimer of the great weariness who taught, 'All is the same, nothing is worth while, the world is without meaning, knowledge strangles." This prophecy concerned bad consequences of widespread belief in the eternal recurrence and caused the dream in which Zarathustra first glimpsed its cosmology. Zarathustra is shocked to see the soothsayer but eventually welcomes him hospitably. Cries of distress are heard from below, leading the soothsayer announces the intention of tempting Zarathustra to his "final sin" of pity.[46] Zarathustra is alarmed, and the soothsayer explains that "the *higher man*" is crying out for him (Z IV: "The Cry of Distress"). Thomas Brobjer (2023) notes that Nietzsche thought of "The Temptation of Zarathustra" as a good title for Part IV (142). This identifies its main antagonist as the soothsayer, who seeks to tempt Zarathustra to give into pity and disrupt his life projects to assuage the distress of the higher men.

The soothsayer then tells him, "Come, come, come! It is time! It is high time!" This is the final use of "high time" [*höchste Zeit*] in the book, and the only one not by Zarathustra's shadow or by Zarathustra himself recalling his shadow's remarks. The phrase indicates the impending beginning of someone's journey toward accepting the eternal recurrence. Earlier it was high time for Zarathustra, and now it is high time for others. The soothsayer then dismisses Zarathustra's claim to happiness, advancing his characteristically gloomy view that "nothing is worth while, no seeking avails, nor are there any blessed isles any more." At this, Zarathustra becomes sure of himself and rejects the soothsayer's claims, saying "*That* I know better: there still are blessed isles. Be quiet

---

[46] See Berry (2024) for more discussion of Nietzsche's critique of pity.

about *that*, you sighing bag of sadness!" Zarathustra then parts from the soothsayer with a prediction: "in the evening we should both be cheerful," and "you yourself shall dance to my songs as my dancing bear" (Z IV: "The Cry of Distress"). Dancing has a significant connection to the eternal recurrence – the animals describe all things as dancing when they proclaim it, and Zarathustra dances with Life before proclaiming it himself. As Robin Small (2010) helpfully suggests, "in dancing, the body affirms itself and its world, rather than seeking compensation in some 'afterworld'" (156). If the soothsayer's victory would consist in making Zarathustra a therapist for pitiable higher men, Zarathustra's victory would consist in making the soothsayer dance and proclaim the eternal recurrence.

Whether blessed isles [*glückseligen Inseln*] exist is equivalent to whether the world around us is rich in value. "Upon the Blessed Isles" discusses how belief in a transcendent God detracts from life by placing value where human will, sensation, and thought can't easily engage with it. Zarathustra says, "Could you create a god? Then do not speak to me of any gods. But you could well create the superhuman." He continues, "Could you *think* a god? But this is what the will to truth should mean to you: that everything be changed into what is thinkable for man, visible for man, feelable by man. You should think through your own senses to their consequences" (Z II: "Upon the Blessed Isles"). Will, thought, and sensation engage more directly and intensely with the worldly than the transcendent. Worldly value therefore enriches life more than transcendent value does. So in disagreeing about the existence of blessed isles, the soothsayer and Zarathustra disagree about whether this world is rich in value. The soothsayer's gloomy philosophy says no; Zarathustra's life-affirming philosophy says yes. Because Zarathustra values the superhuman above all, he identifies the blessed isles with the places where the superhuman can be cultivated. As he says earlier, "My children are still verdant in their first spring, standing close together and shaken by the same winds – the trees of my garden and my best soil. And verily, where such trees stand together there are blessed isles" (Z III: "On Involuntary Bliss"). The existence of the blessed isles, therefore, would suggest saying "Yes" to the eternal recurrence, while their nonexistence would suggest saying "No."

Zarathustra meets a motley collection of higher men on his morning journey down the mountain. He invites each of them back to his cave for dinner. When he returns to his cave late in the afternoon, he hears another cry of distress coming from it. This cry comes from the higher men, who have all accepted Zarathustra's dinner invitation and are crying out for him from his cave. In addition to the soothsayer, there are two kings, the ass carrying the kings' supplies, a conscientious neuroscientist of leeches, a deceptive magician, a pope who retired because God died, the ugliest man (who killed God), a vegetarian beggar who befriends cows, and Zarathustra's shadow.[47]

The higher men aren't the best guests. The eagle is between them, "bristling and restless, for he had been asked too many questions for which his pride had no answer; and the wise serpent hung around his neck" (Z IV: "The Welcome"). Zarathustra tells the higher men, "you are poor company; you who utter cries of distress upset each other's hearts as you sit here together." He however appreciates his own role as the brave one amidst their despair, and offers them his hospitality in thanks.

The king at the right thanks Zarathustra for his hospitality, and explains that the higher men are there because they "have all at once said to their hearts, 'Does Zarathustra still live? Life is no longer worth while, all is the same, all is in vain, or – we must live with Zarathustra.'" The only alternative they see to the soothsayer's gloomy worldview is Zarathustra's life-affirming philosophy, and they want to live with him so that they can be uplifted by it. The king adds that others are coming, saying "this is what is on its way to you: the last remnant of God among men – that is, all the men of great longing, of great nausea, of great disgust, all who do not want to live unless they learn to *hope* again, unless they learn from you, O Zarathustra, the *great* hope" (Z IV: "The Welcome"). He then takes Zarathustra's hand to kiss it.

Zarathustra however resists this veneration and gives the higher men the honest but unwelcoming message that they are not the right men for him. They ask him to alleviate their distress; he needs allies who will help him achieve his goals. He moreover says "no, no, three times no!" to the men whom the king called "the remnant of God," telling the assembled higher men that he awaits "those who are higher, stronger, more triumphant, and more cheerful," whom he calls "*laughing lions*" (Z IV: "The Welcome"). The book will end with Zarathustra leaving the higher men the next morning, when a laughing lion comes to Zarathustra's cave. Peter Berkowitz (1995) takes Zarathustra's departure to repudiate the views that he and the higher men endorse during the night's festivities. But here Zarathustra reveals that he is committed to departing regardless of the night's events, as he doesn't want to spend his life doing therapy for distressed higher men.

Zarathustra then tells them to "Speak to me of my gardens, of my blessed isles" and "This present I beseech from your love, that you speak to me of my children." Returning to arboreal metaphors, he calls the children he hopes for "this living plantation, these life-trees of my will and my highest hope!" At this all are silent, and "only the old soothsayer made signs and gestures with his

---

[47] Santaniello (2018) discusses these characters in detail.

hands" (Z IV: "The Welcome"). We might imagine him optimistic about winning his debate with Zarathustra, as none of the higher men speak of these children or suggest that the blessed isles remain. Whether the higher men are insulted into silence by Zarathustra's criticisms is left unclear.

The soothsayer breaks the silence by asking for dinner to be served, along with wine. The king at the left replies that they have brought "wine enough – a whole ass-load" (Z IV: "The Last Supper"). Feasting, drinking, singing, and philosophy ensue. The section title and the text explicitly compare their dinner party to the Biblical last supper. Including Zarathustra, the higher men, the eagle, the serpent, and the ass, the number of attendees is thirteen, the same as the Biblical feast. The animals are rightly enumerated among the attendees. Zarathustra often steps out of the cave to speak privately to his eagle and serpent when the higher men annoy him. The braying of the ass will have its own philosophical significance.

Despite Zarathustra's annoyance with the higher men, he soon becomes happy that they are overcoming the unhappiness that caused their cries of distress. Despite stepping outside his cave to be away from them, "he enjoyed their gaiety. For this seemed to him a sign of convalescence" (Z IV: "The Awakening" 1). He then tells his animals, "This day represents a triumph: he is even now retreating, he is fleeing, *the spirit of gravity*, my old archenemy." Hearing the higher men's laughter from within his cave, he reiterates, "They are biting, my bait is working: from them too their enemy retreats, the spirit of gravity." Zarathustra is happy to see the higher men convalescing, though he will be surprised about where this takes them.

13 "The Ass Festival" Celebrates Worldly Value

Zarathustra then is astonished to see the higher men begin worshipping the ass like a god. The ugliest man recites "a pious strange litany to glorify the adored and censed ass," and the other higher men kneel in worship. The last of the eight verses praises the animal appetites of the ass: "You love she-asses and fresh figs; you do not despise food. A thistle tickles your heart if you happen to be hungry. In this lies the wisdom of a god" (Z IV: "The Awakening" 2).

After each verse, the ass replies "Yeah-Yuh" (Z IV: "The Awakening" 2). This is a translation of *I-A*, expressing the sound donkeys make in German, for which the donkey-English translation is "hee-haw." It also sounds like *ja*, meaning "yes." While the ass has brayed it a few times before, "Yea-Yuh" has been heard only once in *Zarathustra* as the product of a human mouth. Earlier Zarathustra criticized those who consider everything good and this world the best. Such men I call the omni-satisfied. Omni-satisfaction, which knows how to taste everything, that is not the best taste. I honor the recalcitrant choosy tongues and stomachs, which have learned to say 'I' and 'yes' and 'no.' But to chew and digest everything – that is truly the swine's manner. Always to bray Yea-Yuh – that only the ass has learned, and whoever is of his spirit. (Z III: "On the Spirit of Gravity 2")

Here, the higher men worship an ass that says Yea-Yuh. Zarathustra's reaction is as negative as his previous remark suggests.

Zarathustra leaps back into his cave with a mocking "Yeah-Yuh," louder than that of the ass. Pulling the higher men up from the floor where they are praying, he tells them that "Everyone would judge that with your new faith you were the worst blasphemers or the most foolish of all little old women" (Z IV: "The Ass Festival" 1). Zarathustra demands that they justify their behavior.

First he asks the retired pope, "how do you reconcile this with yourself that you adore an ass in this way as a god?" The pope emphasizes his theological expertise and replies, "Better to adore God in this form than in no form at all!" He continues, "He who said, 'God is a spirit,' took the biggest step and leap to disbelief that anybody has yet taken on earth: such a saying can hardly be redressed on earth. My old heart leaps and jumps that there is still something on earth to adore." Zarathustra then asks the scientist, "doesn't anything here go against your conscience? Is your spirit not too clean for such praying and the haze of these canters?" To the question of how worshipping God is consistent with his empiricist principles, the conscientious scientist answers, "Perhaps I may not believe in God; but it is certain that God seems relatively most credible to me in this form" (Z IV: "The Ass Festival" 1).

Both the retired pope and the conscientious scientist answer Zarathustra by recalling his emphasis of the worldly over the transcendent. The ass doesn't pretend to be anything more than a worldly being, and provides a starkly comical contrast with a transcendent God. This accords with Zarathustra's advice to "no longer to bury one's head in the sand of heavenly things, but to bear it freely, an earthly head, which creates a meaning for the earth" (Z I: "On the Afterworldly"). The pope emphasizes that the donkey is something worldly to adore, while the scientist contrasts the strong empirical evidence for the ass with the lack of empirical evidence for a transcendent God.

The ugliest man is the murderer of God, and Zarathustra interrogates him last. (He also poses questions to the magician and the shadow, but their answers are shorter and somewhat less significant for present matters.) As the ugliest man lies on the ground offering wine to the ass, Zarathustra asks why he fell back into a form of worship, and brought God back to life: "Is it true what they say, that you have wakened him again? And why? Had he not been killed and finished for a reason?" The ugliest man replies by recalling Zarathustra's own advice from "On Reading and Writing": "'Not by wrath does one kill, but by laughter' – thus you once spoke" (Z IV: "The Ass Festival" 1).

Impressed by these answers, Zarathustra accepts that the higher men are right. First, he joins the scientist and the pope in emphasizing the worldly over the transcendent. He expresses this point by parodying Jesus: "except ye become as little children, ye shall not enter into *that* kingdom of heaven. (And Zarathustra pointed upward with his hands.) But we have no wish whatever to enter into the kingdom of heaven: we have become men – so *we want the earth*" (Z IV: "The Ass Festival" 2).

Zarathustra then agrees with the ugliest man about the pragmatic value of laughter for convalescing from religious faith. He tells them, "you have all blossomed; it seems to me such flowers as you are require *new festivals*, a little brave nonsense, some divine service and ass festival," Zarathustra encourages the higher men to celebrate the ass festival again, acknowledging its role in their convalescence, and encouraging them to do it "in remembrance of *me*" (Z IV: "The Ass Festival" 3). This again parodies Jesus, who shares bread with disciples and calls it his body while telling them, "Do this in remembrance of Me" (*Luke* 22:19). Any subsequent ass festivals will parody Catholic Mass, endorsed by Zarathustra parodying Jesus.

Peter Berkowitz writes that Zarathustra "calls into question his love for and reconciliation with eternity" with his "descent to the humiliating depths of ass worship" (223). According to Berkowitz, Zarathustra's endorsement of "abject ass worship" discredits his "announcement that God is dead, his revelation of the superman, his articulation of the ethics of creativity, and his attempt to make himself a god" (226). Following Leo Strauss (1983), Berkowitz finds a *reductio ad absurdum* of Zarathustra's stated views in "the ass worship in which he takes a leading role" (222).

The higher men's advocacy of ass worship over God worship is however more convincing than Berkowitz's sentiments to the contrary. The crucial point comes from the conscientious scientist: There is decisive empirical evidence for the existence of the ass, while empirical evidence (especially in the form of the problem of evil) strongly suggests the nonexistence of God. On standard naturalistic views, God worshippers have lost track of their empirical evidence and deluded themselves into venerating a nonexistent being, while ass worshippers venerate something for which there is strong empirical evidence. The retired pope and the ugliest man's remarks gain significance from the conscientious scientist's naturalism. God's nonexistence prevents anyone who adores Him from having genuine interactions with Him, while the ass exists and can be adored as the pope suggests. Moreover, while God can't improve human life because He doesn't exist, the ass can improve human life because he does exist. And while there may be things intrinsically more fit for worship than donkeys, the ugliest man's point that laughter helps people overcome erroneous religious faith gives ass worship distinctive instrumental value. Naturalism suggests that Berkowitz' disdainful view is mistaken, and the higher men are right.

The Ass Festival itself recalls the medieval Feast of the Ass, a subversive Mass celebrated in medieval Europe from the eleventh to fifteenth centuries.[48] As practiced in Beauvais, France, it began with a young woman and a small child riding a donkey to St. Stephen's Church for Mass, to honor the donkey that carried Mary and the baby Jesus to Egypt. Nietzsche later demonstrates awareness of this tradition: "There is a point in every philosophy when the philosopher's 'conviction' appears on the stage – or to use the language of an ancient Mystery: *adventavit asinus, pulcher et fortissimus*" (BGE 6). The Latin words mean "the ass arrived, beautiful and most brave." In Beauvais, they were the first words of a song to honor the ass when it arrived at Mass, much like the litany recited by the ugliest man. Instead of thanking God three times at the end of Mass, the assembled audience would hee-haw three times (in donkey-French, *hinham*). Catholic authorities frowned on this irreverent celebration, and suppressed it in the 1400s. While "The Seven Seals" reverses the apocalyptic message of *Revelation*, "The Ass Festival" reverses the solemn gravity of traditional Catholic Mass, continuing the parodic whimsy of The Feast of the Ass.

Zarathustra and the higher men then walk out into the cool night. There the ugliest man declares, "Living on earth is worth while: one day, one festival with Zarathustra, taught me to love the earth. 'Was that life?' I want to say to death. 'Well then! Once more!'" (Z IV: "The Drunken Song" 1). These are the same words – *War das das Leben? Wohlan! Noch Ein Mal!* – that Zarathustra used to illustrate a courageous acceptance of recurrence in "On the Vision and the Riddle." Though only a single cycle of recurrence is requested rather than infinite cycles, the positive value ascribed to life implies that the eternal recurrence will have infinite value. Hearing the ugliest man's question, the higher men become overcome with emotion, some thanking Zarathustra and others laughing and crying.

Zarathustra predicted that the old soothsayer would be cheerful in the evening and dance. The prediction comes true: "the old soothsayer was dancing with joy; and even if, as some of the chroniclers think, he was full of sweet wine, he was certainly still fuller of the sweetness of life and he had renounced all weariness" (Z IV: "The Drunken Song" 1). The story that began with the

---

[48] Crowley (1913). Higgins (1987) finds additional parallels to Apuleius' *The Golden Ass.*

soothsayer's prophecy of the great weariness, which led Zarathustra to his first glimpse of the eternal recurrence, now ends triumphantly. The soothsayer renounces weariness and accepts the eternal recurrence.

The ass partakes in the festivities, possibly celebrating the eternal recurrence. Nietzsche writes, "There are even some who relate that the ass danced too, and that it had not been for nothing that the ugliest man had given him wine to drink before." Then after the first stroke of the midnight bell, "everything listened, even the ass and Zarathustra's animals of honor, the eagle and the serpent" (Z IV: "The Drunken Song" 2).

Calling everyone to wander into the night, Zarathustra makes a final speech to them with a commentary on "Once More." While the song and his commentary were discussed in Section 10, what remains to be noted is how his joy makes him evaluate omni-satisfaction more favorably. Before his battle with his abysmal thought and his convalescence, he honored the "choosy tongues and stomachs" over those who "bray Yeah-Yuh" like the ass (Z III: "On the Spirit of Gravity" 2). But with joy making him wish for everything to recur eternally, he forms favorable attitudes toward all things:[49]

> Have you ever said Yes to a single joy? O my friends, then you said Yes too to *all* woe. All things are entangled, ensnared, enamored; if ever you wanted one thing twice, if ever you said, 'You please me, happiness! Abide, moment!' then you wanted *all* back. All anew, all eternally, all entangled, ensnared, enamored – oh, then you *loved* the world. Eternal ones, love it eternally and evermore; and to woe too, you say: go, but return! *For all joy wants – eternity.* (Z IV: "The Drunken Song" 10).

As mentioned in the previous discussion of "Once More," all joy justifies instrumental desires for the eternal recurrence of all things, to bring joy back again.

If joy is deeper than agony in being more plentiful, it can redeem all agony by making up for it. This makes the eternal recurrence of all good and bad things an infinitely good outcome. Zarathustra tells the higher men, "so rich is joy that it thirsts for woe, for hell, for hatred, for disgrace, for the cripple, for world – this world, oh, you know it!" Even here he doesn't forget the criticisms that will soon motivate his departure, saying "You higher men, for you it longs, joy, the intractable blessed one – for your woe, you failures." But to will the eternal recurrence out of joy is even to will all failure again, and as he tells them, "You higher men, do learn this, joy wants eternity. Joy wants the eternity of *all* things,

---

[49] As he writes, "My formula for greatness in a human being is *amor fati:* that one wants nothing to be different, not forward, not backward, not in all eternity" (EH "Clever" 10). Young (2010) and Han-Pile (2011) liken *amor fati* to eternal recurrence; Loeb (2021) distinguishes them.

wants deep, wants deep eternity" (Z IV: "The Drunken Song" 11). Then the higher men and Zarathustra sing "Once More."

Zarathustra concludes with this night of celebration and Zarathustra's departure the next morning. Some regard Part IV as anticlimactic, and perhaps it is after the sevenfold song of love for Eternity that ends Part III.[50] It is also a stylistic outlier, even in a stylistically varied book. But in giving us a new perspective on ideas expressed differently earlier in the book, it helps us understand *Zarathustra* and Nietzsche's broader philosophy. Additional textual evidence is welcome when trying to decipher the rich and complicated images and symbols throughout the book. This makes Part IV valuable for those wishing to understand Parts I–III, as well as those like myself who appreciate it for its own sake.

The narrative structure of Part IV engages with the central themes of *Zarathustra* – the eternal recurrence, and the value of life. Its central conflict is the philosophical battle between Zarathustra and the soothsayer. The soothsayer would win by seducing Zarathustra to his final sin of pity for the higher man. This would be an implicit admission that life is bad, and that there is nothing better to do than to make the burden of life more bearable for others. The eternal recurrence would make this burden infinitely heavy.

Zarathustra wins when the soothsayer wishes for recurrence along with all the other higher men. He fulfills his animals' description of him as *"teacher of the eternal recurrence"* (Z III: "The Convalescent"). At least for one drunken night, the soothsayer accepts that life is worth living again. The other higher men all recognize that life is good and worth living again. Zarathustra might describe what they recognize as the existence of the blessed isles, or the beauty of Life. They see the world as rich in value, and worth living in.

Much of Nietzsche's philosophy explores the value of the forms can take after the death of God. Even if there is no objective value, the eternal recurrence infinitely multiplies the finite subjective value in one life. Even in a godless world, it gives those well-disposed to life a heavenly existence. As all joy eternally recurs, the finite beauty of Life becomes the infinite beauty of Eternity.

---

[50] Strauss (2017).

Notes on Texts, Translations, and Abbreviations

The following abbreviations and translations of Nietzsche's works are used in this volume. In the references to Nietzsche's works, Roman numerals generally denote the volume number of a set of collected works or the standard subdivision within a single work, and Arabic numerals denote the relevant section number. "Pref" is the abbreviation for the preface to a given work (except for the preface to the 1886 edition of *The Birth*). Page numbers are added when sections are long, providing more precise information about the location of the relevant text. In citing Nietzsche's notes in KSA, references provide the volume number followed by the relevant fragment number. The one exception is KSA 14, in which case the page number is provided.

Abbreviations for Nietzsche's Collected Works in the Original German

KSA *Friedrich Nietzsche: Sämtliche Werke. Kritische Studienausgabe*, eds. G. Colli and M. Montinari, 15 vols. Berlin, New York, Munich: DTV, De Grutyer (1999).

Abbreviations and Translations for Titles of Published Works*

BGE *Jenseits von Gut und Böse* (1886): translated as *Beyond Good and Evil*. In *Beyond Good and Evil*, trans. Walter Kaufmann. New York: Vintage (1989).

BT *Die Geburt der Tragödie* (1872/1886); translated as *The Birth of Tragedy*. In *The Birth of Tragedy and the Case of Wagner*, trans. W. Kaufmann, 15–151. New York: Vintage (1967).

D *Morgenröthe* (1881/1887); translated as *Daybreak*. In *Daybreak*, ed. M. Clark and B. Leiter, trans. R. J. Hollingdale. Cambridge: Cambridge University Press (1997).

GM *Zur Genealogie der Moral* (1887); translated as *On the Genealogy of Morals*. In *On the Genealogy of Morals and Ecce Homo*, trans. W. Kaufmann, 13–163. New York: Random House (1989).

GS *Die fröhliche Wissenschaft* (1882/1887); translated as *The Gay Science*. In *The Gay Science*, trans. W. Kaufmann. New York: Vintage Books (1974).

---

* Dates are years of publication.

TI   *Götzen-Dämmerung* (1888); translated as *Twilight of the Idols*. In *The Portable Nietzsche*, ed. and trans. W. Kaufmann, 463–564. New York: Viking Press (1954). References include an abbreviated chapter title and section number.

Z   *Also sprach Zarathustra* (1883–1885; part IV was only distributed privately during Nietzsche's lifetime); translated as *Thus Spoke Zarathustra*. In *The Portable Nietzsche*, ed. and trans. W. Kaufmann, 109–439. New York: Viking Press (1954). References include part number (I-IV), abbreviated chapter title, and section number if relevant.

Abbreviations and Translations for Private Publications, Authorized Manuscripts, and Unpublished Works**

EH   *Ecce Homo* (1888); translated as *Ecce Homo*. In *On the Genealogy of Morals and Ecce Homo*, trans. Walter Kaufmann, 215–335. New York: Random House (1998). References include abbreviated chapter title and section number; in the chapter "Books," the section number is preceded by the abbreviation of the relevant book title.

Abbreviations and Translations for Nietzsche's Unpublished Notebooks

CWFN 6   *Unpublished Fragments from the Period of The Joyful Science (Spring 1881-Summer 1882)*, trans. Adrian Del Caro. In *The Complete Works of Friedrich Nietzsche*, eds. A. D. Schrift and D. Large, vol. 15. Stanford: Stanford University Press (2022).

WP   *Der Wille zur Macht* (1883–1888); translated as *The Will to Power*. In *The Will to Power*, ed. W. Kaufmann, trans. W. Kaufmann and R. J. Hollingdale. New York: Vintage (1968).

** Dates are years of composition.

References

Alfano, Mark (2019). *Nietzsche's Moral Psychology*. New York: Cambridge University Press.

Anderson, Lanier (2005). "Nietzsche on Truth, Illusion, and Redemption." *European Journal of Philosophy*, 13(2): 185–225.

Ansell-Pearson, Keith (1991). "Translations from Nietzsche's Nachlass 1881–1884." *Journal of Nietzsche Studies*, 1: 5–14.

Ansell-Pearson, Keith (2000). "Nietzsche's Brave New World of Force." *Pli*, 9: 6–35.

Askell, Amanda (2018). *Pareto Principles in Infinite Ethics*. Dissertation, New York University.

Benham, William (1887). *The Dictionary of Religion*. London: Cassell.

Berkowitz, Peter (1995). *Nietzsche: The Ethics of an Immoralist*. Cambridge, MA: Harvard University Press.

Berry, Jessica (2024). "'*Poor Mankind! –*': Reexamining Nietzsche's Critique of Compassion." *Inquiry: An Interdisciplinary Journal of Philosophy* 67(5): 1220–1248.

Bocchieri, Pietro, and Angelo Loinger (1957). "Quantum Recurrence Theorem." *Physical Review*, 107: 337–338.

Boltzmann, Ludwig (1896). "Entgegnung auf die Wärmetheoretischen Betrachtungen des Hrn. E. Zermelo." *Annalen der Physik*, 57: 773–784.

Brobjer, Thomas (2023). *The Close Relationship between Nietzsche's Two Most Important Books*. Cham: Springer.

Brush, Stephen (1976). *The Kind of Motion We Call Heat*. Amsterdam: Elsevier.

Burnham, Douglas, and Martin Jesinghausen (2010). *Nietzsche's Thus Spoke Zarathustra*. Edinburgh: Edinburgh University Press.

Capek, Milic (1960). "The Theory of Eternal Recurrence in Modern Philosophy of Science, with Special Reference to C. S. Peirce." *Journal of Philosophy*, 57: 289–296.

Carathéodory, Constantin (1919). "Über den Wiederkehrsatz von Poincaré." *Berl. Sitzungsber*, 34(1919): 580–584.

Caroll, Sean (2019). "Nietzsche: Long Live Physics!" www.preposterousuni verse.com/blog/2009/02/10/nietzsche-long-live-physics/.

Clark, Maudemarie (1990). *Nietzsche on Truth and Philosophy*. Cambridge: Cambridge University Press.

Crowley, Timothy J. (1913). "Feast of Asses." In *Catholic Encyclopedia*, ed. C. Herbermann, 2143–2145. New York: Robert Appleton.

D'Iorio, Paolo (2014). "The Eternal Return: Genesis and Interpretation." *Lexicon Philosophicum: International Journal for the History of Texts and Ideas*, 2: 41–96.

Danto, Arthur (1965). *Nietzsche as Philosopher*. New York: MacMillan.

Deleuze, Gilles (1983). *Nietzsche and Philosophy*, trans. Hugh Tomlinson. New York: Cambridge University Press.

Dombowsky, Don (1997). "The Rhetoric of Legitimation: Nietzsche's 'Doctrine' of Eternal Recurrence." *Journal of Nietzsche Studies*, 14: 26–45.

Drochon, Hugo (2016). *Nietzsche's Great Politics*. Princeton, NJ: Princeton University Press.

Edwards, Phil (2015). "On Hurdy-Gurdy Facts and Fictions." https://crooked timber.org/2015/07/20/hurdy-gurdy-facts-and-fictions/#comment-637220.

Ekonomou, Andrew (2007). *Byzantine Rome and the Greek Popes*. Lanham, MD: Lexington Books.

Fogarty, Matthew (2022). "The Falconer Is Dead: Reassessing Representations of Eternal Recurrence." *International Yeats Studies*, 6(1): 56–72.

Frieman, Joshua, Michael Turner, and Dragan Huterer (2008). "Dark Energy and the Accelerating Universe." *Annual Reviews of Astronomy and Astrophysics*, 46: 385–432.

Gonzáles, Justo (2010). *The Story of Christianity*. New York: HarperCollins.

Gooding-Williams, Robert (2001). *Zarathustra's Dionysian Modernism*. Stanford, CA: Stanford University Press.

Goodsell, Zachary (2024). "Decision Theory Unbound." *Noûs*, 58(3): 669–695.

Gori, Pietro (2019). *Nietzsche's Pragmatism*, ed. and trans. Sarah de Sanctis. Berlin: Walter De Gruyter.

Greene, Brian (2011). *The Hidden Reality*. New York: Vintage.

Han-Pile, Béatrice (2011). "Nietzsche and Amor Fati." *European Journal of Philosophy*, 19: 224–261.

Hatab, Lawrence (2005). *Nietzsche's Life Sentence*. New York: Routledge.

Heidegger, Martin (1991). *Nietzsche, Volumes 1 and 2*, ed. and trans. David Krell. San Francisco, CA: HarperOne.

Higgins, Kathleen (1987). *Nietzsche's Zarathustra*. Philadelphia, PA: Temple University Press.

Huddleston, Andrew (2022). "Affirmation, Admirable Overvaluation, and the Eternal Recurrence." In *Nietzsche on Morality and the Affirmation of Life*, ed. D. Came, 131–153. Oxford: Oxford University Press.

Janaway, Christopher (2022). "Zarathustra's Response to Schopenhauer." In *The Cambridge Critical Guide to Nietzsche's Thus Spoke Zarathustra*, eds. K. Ansell-Pearson and P. Loeb, 83–103. Cambridge: Cambridge University Press.

Jenkins, Scott (2012). "Time and Personal Identity in Nietzsche's Theory of Eternal Recurrence." *Philosophy Compass*, 7(3): 208–217.

Katsafanas, Paul (2022). "What Makes the Affirmation of Life Difficult?" In *The Cambridge Critical Guide to Nietzsche's Thus Spoke Zarathustra*, eds. K. Ansell-Pearson and P. Loeb, 62–82. Cambridge: Cambridge University Press.

Kaufmann, Walter (1968). *Nietzsche: Philosopher, Psychologist, Antichrist*. New York: Vintage.

Korman, Daniel (2015). *Objects*. New York: Oxford University Press.

Krueger, Joe (1978). "Nietzschean Recurrence as a Cosmological Hypothesis." *Journal of the History of Philosophy*, 16: 435–444.

Lampert, Laurence (1986). *Nietzsche's Teaching*. New Haven, NH: Yale University Press.

Langsam, Harold (1997). "How to Combat Nihilism: Reflections on Nietzsche's Critique of Morality." *History of Philosophy Quarterly*, 14: 235–253.

Leiter, Brian (2019). *Moral Psychology with Nietzsche*. Oxford: Oxford University Press.

Lewis, David (1986). *On the Plurality of Worlds*. Oxford: Blackwell.

Loeb, Paul (2010). *The Death of Nietzsche's Zarathustra*. Cambridge: Cambridge University Press.

Loeb, Paul (2015). "The Rebirth of Nietzsche's Zarathustra." *The Agonist*, 8 (1–2): 1–20.

Loeb, Paul (2018). "The Colossal Moment in Nietzsche's Gay Science 341." In *The Nietzschean Mind*, ed. P. Katsafanas, 428–447. Oxfordshire: Routledge.

Loeb, Paul (2021). "Ecce Superhomo." In *Nietzsche's "Ecce Homo,"* eds. N. Martin and D. Large, 207–233. Berlin: De Gruyter.

Loeb, Paul (2022). "What Does Nietzsche Mean by 'the Same' in His Theory of Eternal Recurrence?" *Journal of Nietzsche Studies*, 53(1):1–33.

Löwith, Karl (1997). *Nietzsche's Philosophy of the Eternal Recurrence of the Same*, trans. Harvey Lomax. Berkeley, CA: University of California Press.

Magnus, Bernd (1978). *Nietzsche's Existential Imperative*. Bloomington, IN: Indiana University Press.

McNeil, Bevis (2020). *Nietzsche and Eternal Recurrence*. London: Palgrave McMillan.

Meyer, Matthew (2022). "Nietzsche's Naturalism and Thus Spoke Zarathustra." In *The Cambridge Critical Guide to Nietzsche's Thus Spoke Zarathustra*, eds. K. Ansell-Pearson and P. Loeb, 104–124. Cambridge: Cambridge University Press.

Meyer, Matthew (2024). *The Routledge Guidebook to Nietzsche's Thus Spoke Zarathustra*. Oxfordshire: Routledge.

Mitchell, Jonathan (2021). *Emotion as Feeling Towards Value*. Oxford: Oxford University Press.

Mollison, James. (2021). "Nietzsche's Functional Disagreement with Stoicism: Eternal Recurrence, Ethical Naturalism, and Teleology." *History of Philosophy Quarterly*, 38(2): 175–200.

Mollison, James (2023). "Gilles Deleuze's Interpretation of the Eternal Return." In *Deleuze and Time*, eds. R. Luzecky and D. Smith, 75–97. Cambridge (UK): Edinburgh University Press.

Nehamas, Alexander (1985). *Nietzsche, Life as Literature*. Cambridge, MA: Harvard University Press.

Neves, Juliano (2019). "Nietzsche for Physicists." *Philosophia Scientiæ*, 23(1): 185–201.

Nolt, John (2008). "Why Nietzsche Embraced Eternal Recurrence." *History of European Ideas*, 34(3): 310–323.

Page, Don (1994). "Information Loss in Black Holes and/or Conscious Beings?" *arXiv*. https://arxiv.org/abs/hep-th/9411193.

Parfit, Derek (1984). *Reasons and Persons*. Oxford: Oxford University Press.

Pfeffer, Rose (1965). "Eternal Recurrence in Nietzsche's Philosophy." *Review of Metaphysics*, 19(2): 276–300.

Pippin, Robert (1988). "Irony and Affirmation in Nietzsche's Thus Spoke Zarathustra." In *Nietzsche's New Seas*, eds. M. Gillespie and T. Strong, 45–71. Chicago, IL: University of Chicago Press.

Platt, Michael (1988). "What Does Zarathustra Whisper in Life's Ear?" *Nietzsche-Studien*, 17(1): 179–194.

Poellner, Peter (1995). *Nietzsche and Metaphysics*. Oxford: Clarendon Press.

Poincaré, Henri (1890). "Sur le Problème des Trois Corps et les Équations de la Dynamique." *Acta Math*, 13: 1–270.

Rayman, Joshua (2022). "Nietzsche's Early and Late Conceptions of Time and Eternal Recurrence." *History & Theory*, 61(1): 43–70.

Reginster, Bernard (2006). *The Affirmation of Life*. Cambridge, MA: Harvard University Press.

Remhof, Justin (2018). "Nietzsche on Loneliness, Self-Transformation, and the Eternal Recurrence." *Journal of Nietzsche Studies*, 49(2): 194–213.

Remhof, Justin (2021). "Nietzsche: Metaphysician." *Journal of the American Philosophical Association*, 7(1): 117–132.

Ridley, Aaron (1997). "Nietzsche's Greatest Weight." *Journal of Nietzsche Studies*, 14: 19–25.

Robertson, Simon J. (2012). "The Scope Problem – Nietzsche, the Moral, Ethical, and Quasi-Aesthetic." In *Nietzsche, Naturalism, and Normativity*, eds. C. Janaway and S. Robertson, 81–110. Oxford: Oxford University Press.

Rosen, Stanley (1995). *The Mask of Enlightenment: Nietzsche's Zarathustra.* New Haven, CT: Cambridge University Press.

Santaniello, Weaver (2018). *Zarathustra's Last Supper.* Milton Park: Routledge.

Seung, Thomas K. (2005). *Nietzsche's Epic of the Soul.* Lanham, MD: Lexington Books.

Shapiro, Gary (2016). *Nietzsche's Earth: Great Events, Great Politics.* Chicago, IL: University of Chicago Press.

Shepherd, Melanie (2018). "On the Difficult Case of Loving Life: Plato's Symposium and Nietzsche's Eternal Recurrence." *British Journal for the History of Philosophy,* 26(3): 519–539.

Simmel, Georg (1920). *Schopenhauer and Nietzsche.* Urbana, IL: University of Illinois Press.

Sinhababu, Neil (2008). "Possible Girls." *Pacific Philosophical Quarterly,* 89: 254–260.

Sinhababu, Neil (2015). "Zarathustra's Metaethics." *Canadian Journal of Philosophy,* 45(3): 278–299.

Sinhababu, Neil (2022). "Zarathustra's Moral Psychology." In *The Cambridge Critical Guide to Nietzsche's Thus Spoke Zarathustra,* eds. K. Ansell-Pearson and P. Loeb, 148–167. Cambridge: Cambridge University Press.

Sinhababu, Neil & Teng, Kuong Un (2019). Loving the Eternal Recurrence. *Journal of Nietzsche Studies* 50(1): 106–124.

Small, Robin (1991). "Incommensurability and Recurrence: From Oresme to Simmel." *Journal of the History of Ideas, 52*(1): 121–137.

Small, Robin (2010). *Time and Becoming in Nietzsche's Thought.* London: Continuum.

Small, Robin (2017). *Nietzsche in Context.* Milton Park: Routledge.

Soll, Ivan (1973). "Reflections on Recurrence: A Re-Examination of Nietzsche's Doctrine, Die ewige Wiederkehr des Gleichen." In *Nietzsche: A Collection of Critical Essays,* ed. R. Solomon, 322–342. Garden City, NY: Anchor Press.

Solomon, Robert (2003). *Living with Nietzsche.* Oxford: Oxford University Press.

Strauss, Leo (1983). "Note on the Plan of Nietzsche's beyond Good and Evil." In *Studies in Platonic Political Philosophy,* ed. Joseph Cropsey, 174–191. Chicago, IL: University of Chicago Press.

Strauss, Leo (2017). *Leo Strauss on Nietzsche's Thus Spoke Zarathustra,* trans. Richard Velkley. Chicago, IL: University of Chicago Press.

Strong, Tracy (1975). *Friedrich Nietzsche and the Politics of Transfiguration.* Urbana, IL: University of Illinois Press.

Tappolet, Christine (2016). *Emotions, Values, and Agency.* Oxford: Oxford University Press.

Tinsley, David, and Paul Loeb (eds.) (2022). "Translator's Afterword." In *Complete Works of Friedrich Nietzsche, Vol. 15*, 717–797. Stanford, CA: Stanford University Press.

Verhulst, Ferdinand (2012). *Henri Poincaré*. New York: Springer.

von Tevenar, Gudrun (2013). "Zarathustra: That Malicious Dionysian." In *The Oxford Handbook of Nietzsche*, eds. K. Gemes and J. Richardson, 272–297. Oxford: Oxford University Press.

Welshon, Rex (2004). *The Philosophy of Nietzsche*. Montreal: McGill-Queen's University Press.

Whitlock, Greg (1997). "Examining Nietzsche's 'Time Atom Theory' Fragment from 1873." *Nietzsche-Studien*, 26: 350–360.

Wilkinson, Hayden (2023). "Infinite Aggregation and Risk." *Australasian Journal of Philosophy*, 101(2): 340–359.

Williams, Lewis (forthcoming). "Revolutionary Normative Subjectivism." *Australasian Journal of Philosophy*.

Young, Julian (2010). *Friedrich Nietzsche*. Cambridge: Cambridge University Press.

Zamosc, Gabriel (2015). "What Zarathustra Whispers." *Nietzsche Studien*, 44(1): 231–266.

Zamosc, Gabriel (2022). "Joyful Transhumanism: Love and Eternal Recurrence in Nietzsche's Zarathustra." In *The Cambridge Critical Guide to Nietzsche's Thus Spoke Zarathustra*, eds. K. Ansell-Pearson and P. Loeb, 205–224. Cambridge: Cambridge University Press.

Zermelo, Ernst (1896). "Uber einen Satz der Dynamik und die mechanische Warmetheorie." *Annalen der Physik*, 57: 485–494.

Zuboff, Arthur (1973). "Nietzsche and Eternal Recurrence." In *Nietzsche: A Collection of Critical Essays*, ed. R. Solomon, 343–357. Garden City, NY: Anchor Press.

Cambridge Elements ⁼

Philosophy of Friedrich Nietzsche

Kaitlyn Creasy

California State University, San Bernardino

Kaitlyn Creasy is Associate Professor of Philosophy at California State University, San Bernardino. She is the author of *The Problem of Affective Nihilism in Nietzsche* (2020) as well as several articles in nineteenth-century philosophy and moral psychology.

Matthew Meyer

The University of Scranton

Matthew Meyer is Professor of Philosophy at The University of Scranton. He is the author of three monographs: *Reading Nietzsche through the Ancients: An Analysis of Becoming, Perspectivism, and The Principle of Non-Contradiction* (2014), *Nietzsche's Free Spirit Works: A Dialectical Reading* (Cambridge, 2019), and *The Routledge Guidebook to Thus Spoke Zarathustra* (2024). He has also co-edited, with Paul Loeb, *Nietzsche's Metaphilosophy: The Nature, Method, and Aims of Philosophy* (Cambridge, 2019).

About the Series

Friedrich Nietzsche is one of the most important and influential philosophers of the nineteenth century. This Cambridge Elements series offers concise and structured overviews of a range of central topics in his thought, written by a diverse group of experts with a variety of approaches.

Printed in the United States
by Baker & Taylor Publisher Services